SWEET 16

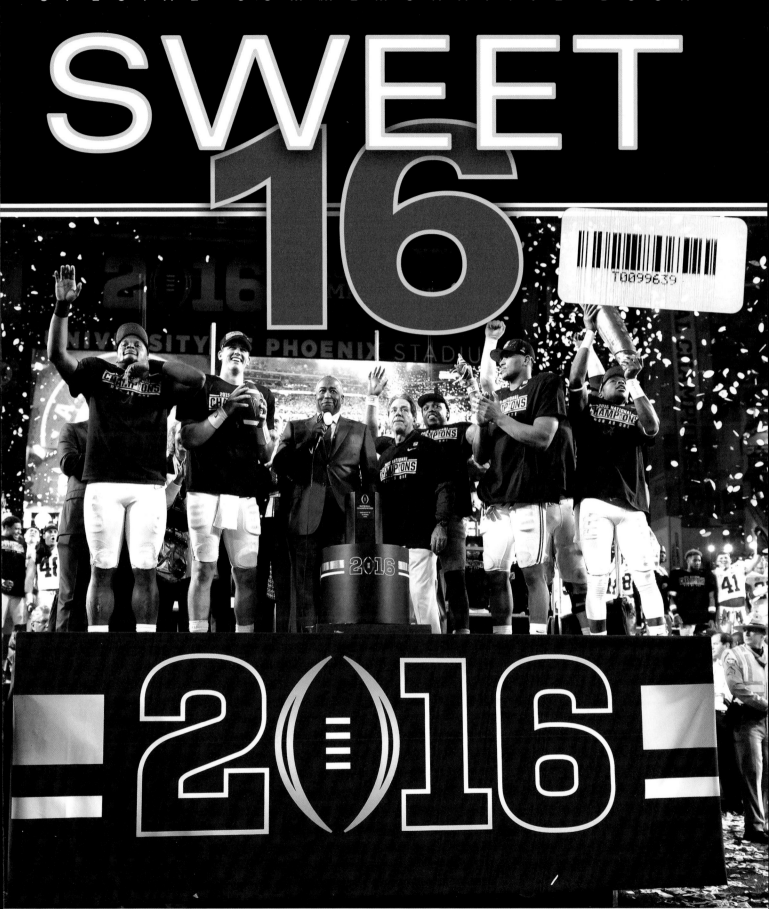

2016

Alabama's Historic 2015 Championship Season

Crimson Tide players celebrate after Alabama defeated Clemson 45-40 to win the program's 16th national championship.

Triumph Books LLC
814 North Franklin Street
Chicago, Illinois 60610
Phone: (312) 337-0747
www.triumphbooks.com

Printed in U.S.A.
ISBN: 978-1-62937-150-4

Content packaged by Mojo Media, Inc.
Joe Funk: Editor
Jason Hinman: Creative Director

All interior and cover photos by AP Images

CONTENTS

ACKNOWLEDGMENTS

A book like this doesn't get done without some serious effort by a lot of people, so special thanks to Noah Amstadter, Tom Bast, and everyone at Triumph Books who contributed.

Because it went to the printer the morning after Alabama's victory in the National Championship Game in order to get it done I had to steal from myself—a lot.

So special thanks to Max Rausch and Bleacher Report (including the editors, etc.) for making that possible. Specifically, I spent the 2015 college football season covering the Southeastern Conference's West Division and the University of Alabama for Bleacher Report, a division of Turner Sports (subsidiary of Time Warner).The digital media company is based in San Francisco.

All of the game stories are re-worked (some more than others) versions of what I wrote during the season, and those stories are listed below. The features are a mishmash of stories I wrote for Bleacher Report and the University of Alabama game programs, often reworked and updated depending on the story. They too are listed below, but if I accidentally forgot to list an excerpt, my apologies.

Finally, as always a special thanks to my wife Megan for her patience and understanding, and the rest of our family including Juno the Wonder Dog and Loki the Dog of Mischief (fellow husky owners will understand).

The following appear here courtesy of Bleacher Report:

- Introduction—includes excerpts from "Alabama's Return to SEC Title Game Nothing Short of Impressive," Nov. 30, 2015, and "What Does Alabama Have to Do to Avoid Another Playoff Letdown?" Dec. 18, 2015

- Ryan Kelly—includes excerpts from: "Alabama's Real Offensive MVP Won't Score a Touchdown This Season," Oct 28, 2015

- Alabama vs. Wisconsin—includes excerpts from "Alabama's Jacob Coker Will Finally Live Up to Expectations in 2015," and "Derrick Henry Poised for Heisman Trophy Run After Monster Week 1," both Sept. 6, 2015

- Alabama vs. Middle Tennessee—"Despite 2-0 Start, Alabama Needs to Quickly Find Its Identity," Sept. 12, 2015

- Alabama vs. Ole Miss—"Self-Destructive Alabama Is in Trouble in the SEC West," Sept. 20, 2015

- Alabama vs. Louisiana-Monroe—"Alabama's Defense Finding Its Groove at the Right Time," Sept. 26, 2015

- Defensive Line—includes excerpts from "Alabama's Sack Attack Unrivaled in College Football," Nov. 18, 2015

- Alabama vs. Georgia—"Alabama Muscles Its Way Back into College Football Playoff Picture," Oct. 3, 2015

- Alabama vs. Arkansas—includes excerpts from "Alabama's Playoff Hopes Rest with Its Ever-Improving Defense," Oct. 11, 2015

- Jake Coker—includes excerpts from "Can Alabama QB Jake Coker Win Between the Hedges at Georgia?" Sept. 28, 2015

- Alabama vs. Texas A&M—"Alabama's Derrick Henry Reminds SEC Why He Must Be Feared," Oct. 17, 2015

- Alabama vs. Tennessee—"Alabama's Close Call vs. Tennessee Exactly What Crimson Tide Needed," Oct. 24, 2015

Alphonse Taylor makes a confetti angel on the University of Phoenix Stadium field after Alabama's win over Clemson in the College Football Playoff Championship Game.

- Defensive Backs—"Alabama's Defensive Backs Making Strides, Showing Notable Improvement from 2014," Oct. 15, 2015

- Remembering Kenny Stabler—"Alabama Pays Tribute to Kenny Stabler Prior to LSU Game," Nov. 7, 2015

- Alabama vs. LSU—"Nick Saban Proves He Owns Les Miles, Has Alabama Playoff Ready," Nov. 8, 2015

- Alabama vs. Mississippi State—"2015 Heisman Trophy Is Now Derrick Henry's to Lose," Nov. 14, 2015

- Alabama's Unsung Heroes—"Alabama's Unsung Inspiration, Michael Nysewander," Dec. 23, 2015

- Alabama vs. Charleston Southern—"Alabama's Focused Domination Proves It Has Tunnel Vision on National Title," Nov. 21, 2015

- Iron Bowl vs. Auburn—"Alabama RB Derrick Henry Locks Up Heisman in Record Breaking Night vs. Auburn," Nov. 28, 2015

- SEC Championship Game vs. Florida—"Alabama Is Way More Than Derrick Henry, Which Should Scare Everyone Else," Dec. 5, 2015

Game stories from the Cotton Bowl and National Championship Game are also courtesy of Bleacher Report.

FOREWORD

By Eli Gold

When we left AT&T Stadium after Week 1 of the 2015 season, the impressive win over Wisconsin, you knew that this Alabama team was good. You just didn't know to what degree. The quarterbacking was still unsettled. We had not seen a ton of Derrick Henry, certainly. Robert Foster was still playing and Calvin Ridley hadn't established himself.

There were a lot of questions, but yes, you knew it was a good ball club.

But how good?

In a rather perverse way, I think one of the most remarkable things this year that led to Alabama playing for the national championship was the loss to Ole Miss—that might have been one of the best things that happened to this ball club. From that point forward these kids knuckled down, they knew that they were playing in an elimination game every single weekend. One more loss and you weren't going to the SEC Championship Game, you were not going to the playoffs. The margin of error was gone, and this team just grew up.

They found a leader in Jake Coker. They believed in him. He showed how tough he was. Then, of course, one thing led to the next and Henry matured and Ridley came along. ArDarius Stewart caught passes and the defense matured into the absolute best this side of the National Football League. It all seemed to turn both in that loss to Ole Miss and at Georgia in that terrible downpour. All of the sudden everything

clicked and this team came together to become an outstanding ball club.

It just showed me, again— and the coach might slap me—but between last year and this year I think we have seen the two finest coaching performances by Nick Saban and his staff. The man just continues to amaze.

Throughout the season the coach talked all the time about this team's chemistry, and it was true. These guys genuinely liked each other. They played for each other. Anyone around them and the team could see and feel it. I don't care where you work and what you do, whether you're a pipe fitter or a welder, a bus driver or a doctor, if you get along with the people you're working with your day goes by more quickly, you enjoy it, and you do a better job. It's no different with a team sport, and this team was as tightly knit as any.

I think the biggest thing, the most rewarding thing, for the coaches and for those of us who were lucky enough to watch every single down, was just to see how these guys matured and grew, how all the questions were answered by the Cokers of the world and others like Michael Nysewander—who ever knew that you'd be talking regularly about Michael Nysewander and Highway 46?

There were so many great stories with this team, and so many wonderful people you always just hoped for the best with this bunch as the Crimson Tide rolled to yet another national championship. ■

Teammates surround Alabama running back Kenyan Drake after Drake's 95-yard kick return for a touchdown in the fourth quarter. Drake's score gave Alabama a 38-27 lead.

INTRODUCTION

The dynasty was dead.

Nick Saban had peaked at the University of Alabama.

The Southeastern Conference's days of domination were over.

That's what fans of every other college football team thought, hoped, and, yes, some even prayed, yet were not close to being correct.

While the rest of the college football world spent most of 2015 thinking that a page could finally be turned on Alabama's supremacy in the sport, the Crimson Tide and Co. had other ideas.

During a season that saw it seemingly revisit its past over and over again with familiar plays, situations and circumstances, Alabama won its fourth national championship since 2009 and 16th overall even though the odds of doing so were anything but in its favor.

Yes, Saban had arguably pieced together the strongest collection of talent anyone had seen in quite some time, with an impressive coaching staff to match. But the rest of the teams in the Southeastern Conference's West Division had upped their status as well, with those in the East desperate to narrow the gap.

Through facility upgrades, higher salaries, and revamped recruiting efforts they were all trying to be like the Crimson Tide, with both fans and administrators growing more frustrated by the continual lack of success. Sure Alabama had failed to win the national championship in either 2013 or 2014, but no one else in the league had broken through, resulting in college football's first two non-SEC champions since 2005.

That caused critics to hastily and mistakenly claim that the conference's golden era was at an end. How quickly they forgot.

They ignored the fact that for the first time every team in a division played in a bowl game in 2014, and focused on the subsequent outcomes when the SEC didn't fare well as well as hoped in games that mostly didn't mean anything. It "only" went 7-5.

They shrugged off every West team being ranked during the first few weeks of the 2015 season, which had also never been achieved before in college football. And it didn't seem to register that when two teams from the same division played one of them had to lose.

Specific to the SEC West it meant an automatic 21 losses for the division that went into the 2015 bowl season having lost just 26 total games. The seven teams were 24-3 against non-conference opponents, and a combined 13-2 against the SEC East.

Alabama? The reigning league champion? It was largely written off despite being ranked third in both major preseason polls. The Crimson Tide wasn't picked to win the division during SEC Media Days in July, when due to false hopes and promises rival Auburn got the most votes (and ended up finishing last).

The Crimson Tide didn't have a starting quarterback in place before or after training camp, the offense had to replace eight other starters, and the receiving corps was at best unproven. It fell flat in the 2014 playoffs, which some foolishly believed was more of a statement about the program than just one game. Factor in Alabama's brutal 2015 schedule and the prevailing thought was that there was

Derrick Henry (No. 2) reaches the end zone late in the fourth quarter. The Heisman Trophy winner's 1-yard run gave Alabama a 45-33 lead.

simply too much for the Crimson Tide to overcome.

"We certainly didn't do a good job last year," Saban said. "I felt like our players did not approach the game like a playoff game. They approached it more like a bowl game, which was obviously not our intention, not what we tried to sell to them as far as what they needed to do.

"I think they felt a little entitled when they won the SEC championship."

Consequently, the critics were circling like a bird of prey, saying "The Process" had been passed by, that Saban was making excuses, and Alabama would never be the same after it had uncharacteristically been pushed around by Ohio State in the Sugar Bowl.

They were even louder when Alabama lost for the second straight year to Ole Miss, this time at Bryant-Denny Stadium, 43-37 on Sept. 19.

Yet the season wasn't over, it was just getting going, and when the easiest thing to do would have been to listen to the naysayers, Alabama didn't. It came back with a vengeance.

"Finish. That's our motto," senior linebacker Reggie Ragland said. "That's all we talk about."

Hearing a player say something like that has become cliché in sports, but this group truly embraced the notion. It stemmed from players like Ragland coming back for his senior year, a defensive front seven that has so many contributors that Florida head coach Jim McElwain halfway joked that it should be called a "front 30," and, of course, running back Derrick Henry.

Even after he won college football's highest honor, and gave a 10-miute speech thanking everyone imaginable, during his first interview back on campus Henry revealed that he only had three things on his mind: practicing, figuring out where he's going to take his offensive linemen out to dinner to show his appreciation, and the playoffs.

"I really don't want to talk about Heisman stuff," he said in response to the first question asked. "I want to focus on what we need to do to get ready for Michigan State."

That spoke a lot about the 2015 Crimson Tide and how it was able to overcome so many things including the previous playoff setback that had the feel of a blowout even though it was by just seven points. Alabama was embarrassed by how it lost and it didn't forget.

"I always ask the players—I asked them last year because of the Ole Miss game, I asked them this year because of the Ole Miss game—'How are you going to respond to the loss?' It's a really true test to your character as a man as how you respond when things don't go well," Saban said.

"Everyone can be a front-runner and everyone can respond the right way when things are going your way. But now you have to realize that there's some tough things that you're going to have to do to overcome the adversity that you've created by the way we've played. Are you going to be willing to do that?"

This team was. The players held a team meeting after Ole Miss, which turned out to be the turning point of the season, and subsequently won nine straight games to finish alone atop the division—plus topped its usual opponent in the SEC Championship Game, Florida, in convincing fashion.

"I think the consistency of what he's done year in and year out, it's hard to do in college football," said McElwain, who was Saban's offensive coordinator from 2008-11, during which Alabama lost back-to-back games only once. "The way he has gotten these players to understand, 'Look, that game's over, learn from it, but let's move on forward and get a little bit better.' That's one thing you see is they continually get better year in and year out.

"You know what, it was fun to be a part of to see how he does that."

In 2012, coaching legend Steve Spurrier half-joked at SEC Media Days that winning the conference was tougher than capturing the national championship. The West Division hadn't had a repeat winner since 1993-94, and the league hadn't had a back-to-back champion since Tennessee in 1997-98.

That was until this team, this year. Alabama survived its brutal schedule. It defended the division title and then extended its reign atop the conference. It used all those reasons everyone gave for how the Crimson Tide wouldn't win another championship as motivation for why it could, and why the dynasty was still alive.

"It's all about will and want to," Ragland said. ■

Alabama's O.J. Howard heads to the end zone. Howard, a junior tight end who had not scored since his freshman year, had two touchdowns against Clemson.

COLLEGE FOOTBALL PLAYOFF NATIONAL CHAMPIONSHIP

ALABAMA 45, CLEMSON 40
January 11, 2016 • Glendale, Arizona

CALL OF A LIFETIME

Onside Kick Turns the Tide in Fourth-Quarter Comeback

There were a little under 11 minutes remaining on the clock of the National Championship Game and the University of Alabama had just tied the score when Nick Saban made the call of a lifetime.

With Alabama struggling to stop Clemson quarterback Deshaun Watson and the momentum up for grabs, Saban called for an onside kick in hopes of catching the Tigers by surprise.

It did more than that.

With junior kicker Adam Griffith striking the ball perfectly and redshirt freshman Marlon Humphrey racing to catch it before anyone from the other side could make a play on it, Alabama recovered and went on to survive a wild 45-40 victory at University of Phoenix Stadium for its 16th national championship.

And oh, how sweet it was.

"This is my—I hate to say it—favorite team because I love 'em all," Saban said. "These guys have come so far and have done so much. Their will, their spirit to compete and do the kind of kind of things they needed to do to be the kind of team they could be, I'm happy for them.

"This is all about winning a game for them. It's great for our fans. It's great for the state of Alabama, but I wanted to win this game for these guys."

With it the debate can really begin about if Saban is the greatest coach in college football history, and if Alabama's ongoing dynasty is the best the game has ever seen. The crown was Saban's fifth, his fourth with the Crimson Tide, and Alabama became the first program during the modern era to win four titles over a seven-year span.

Paul W. "Bear" Bryant won six national championships at Alabama, yet three were split titles, and the school claims the 1973 team that lost the No. 1 vs. No. 2 matchup with Notre Dame in the Sugar Bowl.

Saban's only split title was in 2003, when the Associated Press and Football Writers Association of America both voted Southern California No. 1. However, LSU won the game that mattered most, against Oklahoma in the Sugar Bowl, and took home the crystal football.

Additionally, this was Saban's sixth victory against a team ranked No. 1, while no one else in college football history has more than four (Lou Holtz,

>>> **PLAYER OF THE GAME**

Junior tight end O.J. Howard became the receiving threat Alabama always hoped he would, making five receptions for 208 yards and two touchdowns.

Marlon Humphrey celebrates after recovering an onside kick in the fourth quarter. The trick play, which followed an Alabama field goal, proved to be the turning point in Alabama's win over Clemson.

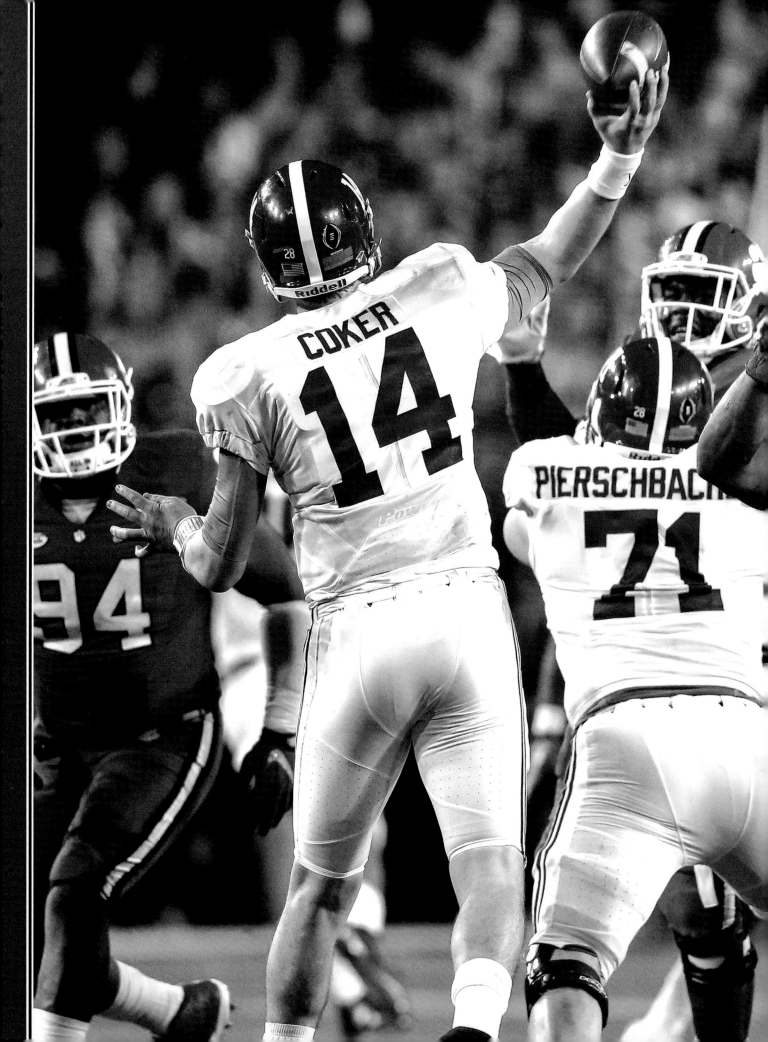

Jimmy Johnson, and Jack Mollenkopf with four; Bryant had three). Alabama extended its streak of being No. 1 at some point in a season to an incredible eight years, and it became the first team in college football history to beat nine ranked opponents en route to a title.

Regardless, after both semifinal games were blowouts the championship more than made up for it and will go down as one of the best title games ever played. The two teams combined for 1,023 yards and it still went down to the very last play.

Junior running back Derrick Henry rushed for 158 yards on 36 carries and scored three touchdowns while becoming Alabama's all-time leading rusher.

Despite being sacked five times senior quarterback Jake Coker had a career high 335 yards on 16 of 25 attempts, and no turnovers.

Overshadowing both was the game's offensive MVP, junior tight end O.J. Howard, who had a historic performance with five receptions for 208 yards and touchdowns of 51 and 53 yards.

"O.J., quite honestly, should have been more involved all year long," Saban said. "Sometimes he was open and we didn't get him the ball, but I think the last two games have been breakout games for him in terms of what he's capable of and what he can do.

"I would say that it's bad coaching on my part that he didn't have the opportunity to do that all year long."

But Saban's decision to go for the onside kick was the one most people were talking about afterward. Many of the Crimson Tide players said it the gutsiest call they'd ever seen.

"That was amazing," senior wide receiver Richard Mullaney said.

Alabama had actually been practicing it since Week 3 of the season. When Saban saw

Jake Coker completed 16 of 25 passes for 335 yards and two touchdowns in Alabama's win over Clemson.

NOTABLE

With 158 rushing yards, Derrick Henry finished with 3,591 career yards to break Shaun Alexander's Alabama record (3,565) despite being a starter for only one season.

how Clemson lined up after Henry opened the scoring with a 50-yard touchdown run he knew it would be an option in the game and waited for the best opportunity.

How many coaches would call it in the fourth quarter with everything on the line?

"It was just a matter of Adam Griffth kicking the ball to the right spot, and us not being offside," said special-teams coach Bobby Williams, who estimated that the play's success rate during practices was about "50-50."

"I almost dropped the ball almost every time," Humphrey said about the misses.

Nevertheless, it helped give Alabama the momentum for good, especially after Howard subsequently scored his 51-yard touchdown for the lead the Crimson Tide would never relinquish.

Although it struggled to slow Watson, who compiled 478 (405 passing and 73 rushing) of his team's 550 total yards, it eventually did just enough.

Safety Eddie Jackson, named the defensive player of the game, picked Watson off in the second quarter to set up Alabama's second touchdown, and freshman safety Ronnie Harrison prevented one with a clutch deflection of a pass into the end zone.

Overall, Alabama accumulated seven tackles for a loss, including two sacks, and broke up seven passes, but the victory took absolutely everything Alabama had. That included a 95-yard kickoff return for a touchdown by senior Kenyan Drake, and junior defensive linemen A'Shawn Robinson and Jarran Reed serving as fullbacks to help Henry punch in his final score, a 1-yard touchdown dive.

Kenyan Drake eludes a Clemson defender as he breaks free to return a kickoff 95 yards for a touchdown in the fourth quarter.

"I'm exhausted," Coker said after lighting up a victory cigar with teammates in the locker room. "We had to earn it, that's for sure."

It was a fitting end for this game and this season, against a team coached by former Alabama player Dabo Swinney. He was known for saying "Bring your own guts," and Clemson certainly did, against the team that appropriately had an elephant mascot.

"We didn't always play pretty in this game," Saban said. "It probably wasn't one of our best games when it comes to flat execution. But when it comes to competing and making plays when we needed to make them, it was probably as good as it gets.

"I think that's the kind of competitors that win championships, and that's probably why we're sitting here [with the trophy]." ∎

Opposite: Clemson quarterback Deshaun Watson loses the ball on a failed two-point conversion attempt late in the fourth quarter. Alabama won despite an amazing performance by the Clemson quarterback, who passed for 405 yards and four touchdowns.
Above: Coach Nick Saban leads the Crimson Tide onto the field before the game.

Derrick Henry dives in to the end zone to score in the second quarter. The 2015 Heisman Trophy winner scored three touchdowns against Clemson.

'IT FELT LIKE A DREAM'

O.J. Howard Catches 2 TDs, Takes Offensive MVP Honors

It was as if the entire University of Alabama fan base briefly said "Finally!" while still trying to hold its collective breath until the very end of the National Championship Game.

O.J. Howard, who despite his 6-foot-6 frame and obvious top-notch receiving skills had previously only made 33 receptions for 394 yards during the 2015-16 season, and hadn't been in the end zone since his freshman year.

That promptly came to an end in a big way, on college football's biggest stage. Not only did the junior tight end score a 51-yard touchdown, but added a 53-yard score while having an unforgettable night.

"Initially it felt like a dream and I tried to tell everybody to wake me up because I thought it wasn't real," Howard said. "It was just a great feeling to get in the end zone again."

Howard eventually finished with five receptions for 208 yards, which set Alabama records for receiving yards by a tight end in a game and receiving yards by anyone in a bowl game (previously held by Ray Perkins, 178 vs. Nebraska in the 1967 Sugar Bowl).

Consequently, he was named the game's offensive MVP, while junior safety Eddie Jackson earned the defensive honor after making his sixth interception of the season.

Although junior running back Derrick Henry finished with 158 rushing yards on 36 carries and three touchdowns, Alabama knew going in that it would need more than a big-time performance from the Heisman Trophy winner to win.

Saban called it "big-little" game, in that Clemson's defense was the kind in which Alabama's offense would have some negative plays (although didn't anticipate having so many), but it would also have the chance to get some playmakers into open space.

"I thought we would be able to make some big plays in this game," he said.

Noticing the Clemson players sometimes needed a while to get lined up as they wanted, part of Alabama's strategy was to go hurry-up. The result was that the Tigers could get into formation, but then would not be able to make adjustments before the snap.

It especially helped Howard get open.

He was essentially left uncovered on both touchdowns, the first giving Alabama its initial lead at 21-14 early in the second half, and the second helping the Crimson Tide pull ahead for good in the fourth quarter, 31-24.

"No safety was over the top," Howard said about the long sideline pass. "I kind of knew that one was going to be open."

Actually, offensive coordinator Lane Kiffin was seen raising his arms for the touchdown as senior quarterback Jake Coker, who had a career-high 335 passing yards on just 16 completions (but no turnovers), released the ball down field.

"We needed that big time," Coker said about the first touchdown, as Saban had noted during his halftime interview that his quarterback was holding on to the ball too long.

"The second one was just the exact same play from last week against Michigan State," Howard said about his 41-yard completion while contributing to the 38-0

O.J. Howard tries to get past Clemson's T.J. Green. Howard was named the Offensive MVP of the National Championship Game after catching five passes for 208 yards.

victory in the Cotton Bowl. "This time I took the middle of the field, nobody was in the middle and it was wide open. Just a great play call by Coach Kiffin."

But Howard's biggest play may have been the 63-yard catch-and-go to set up Alabama's final touchdown, a 1-yard Henry dive that all but put the game out of reach.

"Some of those plays were fast plays," Kiffin said. "We were trying to use that to our advantage and some of our guys were able to make plays."

It wasn't until after Clemson rallied for a final last-minute touchdown and the subsequent onside kick went out of bounds that both coaches and Howard could finally exhale and begin the celebration for its 16th national championship. The game had been that tight.

"This is what we stood up and said at the beginning of the season," Howard said. "We wanted to come out and win a national championship and our team fought hard for that. I'm just so proud of our team, and no team deserved this more than we do." ■

OFFENSIVE LINEMAN

RYAN KELLY

70

Third-Year Starter Anchors Nation's Best Offensive Line

R yan Kelly had heard it before. Being a third-year starter and in his fifth season at the University of Alabama there wasn't much that could classify as being new anymore.

But when strength and conditioning coach Scott Cochran said what he always tells all the seniors on their first day of training camp it got the center thinking.

This was the last time he would be going through the first day of practice with the Crimson Tide, just like he went through the final spring, A-Day, and summer. Every senior at every school goes through something similar, although the word legacy carries some extra weight at a place like Alabama.

"Every day that goes by is the last time you're going to do something," he said. "It's unbelievable how fast the time goes by. My parents always tell me it's only gonna go by faster. (I'm) taking advantage of it, just cherishing every moment I have."

That included SEC Media Days in July, when Kelly was one of three players to represent the Crimson Tide, and on Alabama's Fan Day when he helped lead teammates through drills. They're the kind of honors and responsibilities that often go to the captains at the end of the season, and sure enough he eventually landed that honor.

"Ryan Kelly's great," senior running back Kenyan Drake said. "He's definitely the brick of that offensive line. We definitely need him moving forward in our process of becoming champions again because he is a perfect part in our offensive line and also a senior."

Actually, with sophomore left tackle Cam Robinson the only other returning starter, Kelly was the lone established veteran of the offense. After taking over for Barrett Jones in 2013 he had Arie and Cyrus Kouandjio to his left, with Austin Shepherd and Anthony Steen on his right.

Those other four all spent the 2015 summer in NFL training camps, as did Jones. Meanwhile, Alabama had set a new standard at the center position as every

Ryan Kelly prepares to snap the ball to quarterback Jake Coker during Alabama's Oct. 17 game against Texas A&M.

starter since Saban arrived in 2007— including Antoine Caldwell, William Vlachos, and Jones—was named an All-American.

"It's cliché here, but it is the process," Kelly said. "Everyone wants to talk about it, but it's the real thing. No matter who you bring in we aren't going to change our standards for who you are. This is the 'Bama Way. This is a special place. It's not for everybody to come to.

"I think that is one of the biggest things Coach [Nick] Saban has drilled in is that if you come here, you are a part of something bigger than you. Every guy who has had success here has partaken in that. All the success, the way he recruits—you can't get around [the process], the hard work, the dedication, and he's taught me to be a good person as well."

Although center is considered an important position on any football team there's a lot more to it than snapping the ball and making a block. In addition to being responsible for the line calls he's the one guy other than the quarterback who has to know absolutely everything, from the entire playbook to what personnel the opposition prefers to have on the field when it blitzes.

"Almost all of the best offensive lines that I've seen have an anchor, an experienced center who knows what he's doing, who's on the same page as the quarterback, same wavelength, who knows what's going to happen before it happens," Jones said. "It's important that he's a confident guy who doesn't just kind of guess. When he makes a call, guys know that's the right call, and guys get on the same page."

That's why coaches consider experience at the position to be a cherished commodity, and was the key to Jones moving from left tackle to replace Vlachos after winning the Outland Trophy (best interior lineman) in 2011.

While Kelly never had to switch positions it didn't mean he couldn't have played elsewhere on the line.

"If you can play center you can play anywhere because you know the whole offense," said reserve Bradley Bozeman, who emerged to be the backup center as a freshman in 2014 and filled in for two starts after Kelly

had a sprained knee at Ole Miss.

"We watched film and he helped me through it. Gave me tweaks too. The whole year we prepared for that situation, so when he went down and I came in he had my back."

Robinson got similar help from Kelly when he started at left tackle as a true freshman, just like with the three new starters on the line in 2015: Dominick Jackson, Alphonse Taylor, and Ross Pierschbacher—who told reporters as a redshirt freshman guard "Hopefully, I can be as good as Ryan Kelly someday."

Together the five won the inaugural Joe Moore Award as the best offensive line in college football, and a trophy so big that it made Derrick Henry's Heisman Trophy look tiny in comparison.

While the running back ended up sweeping the major national player of the year honors including the Maxwell and Walter Camp awards, and was clearly Alabama's best player in 2015-16, Kelly may have been just as valuable to the Crimson Tide.

"I'm not going to say he's the MVP of the offense, but I will say that center position is so important in college, especially when you're in an up-tempo offense and doing so much at the line of scrimmage," said Jones, who won the 2012 Rimington Award as the nation's best center.

"It's so vital. His leadership, it's hard to characterize how important it is. I think he's invaluable, and I think he's had a great year so far."

When postseason accolades were being considered Kelly had graded about 84 percent in all games, with five games above 90 percent. He had yielded just four quarterback hurries and no sacks while making 16 knockdown blocks.

That landed him the program's second Rimington Trophy along with consensus All-American status.

"Ryan is like the key to the offensive line," Robinson said. "He's the reason everything goes the way it goes. He's extremely important to what we do as a unit, and he's kind of like the heart and soul.

"My appreciation for Ryan Kelly is through the roof." ∎

Ryan Kelly speaks on media day before the 2015 Cotton Bowl. A fifth-year player, Ryan Kelly was the established veteran on Alabama's talented offensive line, which was awarded the Joe Moore Award as the best offensive line in college football.

ALABAMA 35, WISCONSIN 17
September 5, 2015 • Arlington, Texas

OH HENRY!

Tide Roll Over Badgers behind RB's 3 TDs

Release the beast.

That's what the University of Alabama football team did during its season-opening marquee matchup with Wisconsin at AT&T Stadium. Junior running back Derrick Henry may have only touched the ball 15 times, but he certainly made the most of them while accumulating 159 all-purpose yards and scoring three touchdowns.

"Any time you can look up and see No. 2 running down the field with a whole bunch of guys chasing him, that's an awesome feeling," senior center Ryan Kelly said.

Kelly would get to experience that a lot this season. After a relatively quiet training camp, when most of the attention was focused on the passing game—who would start at quarterback and how would Alabama replace Amari Cooper—Henry showed why some believed he'd be a strong contender for the Heisman Trophy.

Despite being one of nine new starters on the offense, Henry had 13 carries for 147 rushing yards and an 11.3 average against the Badgers. Granted, among the newcomers the coaching staff probably worried the least about Henry, but they also made a point not to overuse him.

That could be crucial for the Crimson Tide's title chances, especially since Wisconsin was the first of seven teams ranked in the preseason Associated Press Top 25 Poll that Alabama had on its regular season schedule, with the potential to face three more in the SEC Championship Game and College Football Playoff.

"Oh man, Derrick the whole game was pretty impressive," senior quarterback Jake Coker said.

After taking handoffs on the first four snaps of the game Henry only needed a seam during the second possession to score a 37-yard touchdown.

"Truly I didn't know it was fourth-and-1," Henry said. "I didn't know. I didn't care. As long as we got the touchdown I was happy."

His second touchdown pretty much broke Wisconsin's spirit. On Alabama's second offensive snap of the second half he went 56 yards, which also put him over the 100-yard mark for the sixth time of his career. Four of those had been in neutral-site games.

The third score he just plowed through the left side for a 2-yard touchdown. After that Wisconsin didn't seem too interested in trying to stop him any more, and Alabama obliged by pulling him later in the third quarter.

"That's what we expect out of him and he played a real good game," said senior linebacker Reggie Ragland, who has to face Henry every day in practice. "It's tough."

Wisconsin lost starting safety Michael Caputo, the team co-captain who led the Badgers in tackles in 2014 with 106. After being run over by Henry, he was seen trying to line up on Alabama's side of the field before

>>> PLAY OF THE GAME

Although Henry's second touchdown pretty much put the game away early in the third quarter, senior Kenyan Drake's score was the one to make the highlight reels after he spun out of what should have been a tackle in the backfield and scored a 43-yard touchdown.

Derrick Henry breaks multiple tackles en route to a first-half touchdown. Henry scored three touchdowns in Alabama's season-opening win over Wisconsin.

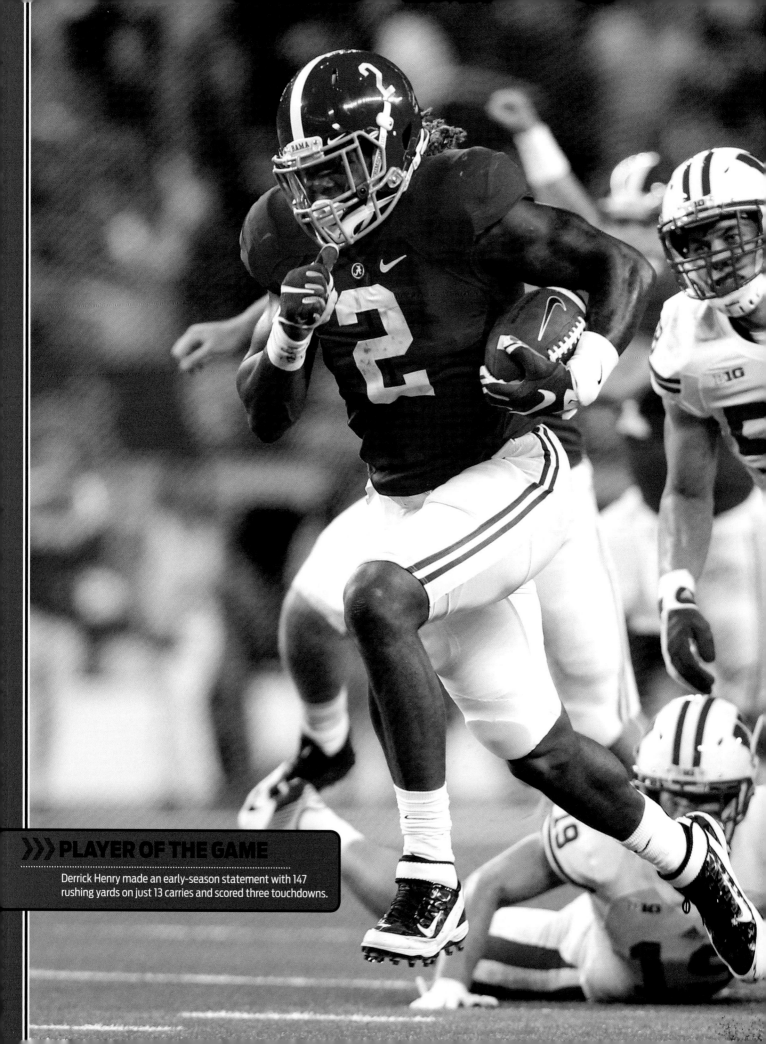

he could be pulled with what was believed to be a concussion.

Notably, Henry scored all three touchdowns while going to his left, which was obviously the strength of the revamped line. Between Kelly and sophomore left tackle Cam Robinson, Ross Pierschbacher made a strong first impression at guard.

"He was awesome," Kelly said. "I think everyone kind of forgets that he's just a redshirt freshman, it was his first game starting and had never played in a game before that. I was kind of a backup and kind of transitioned into a starting role.

"He has a lot of power and great potential."

Also making his first collegiate start was fifth-year quarterback Coker, who had transferred in the previous year from Florida State. After Alabama had a five-man competition during the summer and training camp the decision came down to the senior or sophomore Cooper Bateman.

Saban said he didn't make up his mind about who would take the first snaps until Thursday, and Coker wasn't told about it until meeting with the coach on Friday. No announcement was ever made, not even in the locker room.

"I was the only person he told and no one else knew," Coker said. "I kept it a secret. My parents knew, but they didn't tell anybody."

Regardless, he completed 15 of 21 passes for 213 yards, with one touchdown and no interceptions before Bateman got his chance in the third quarter.

"He did a really good job," Saban said. "I thought he was accurate with the ball, he didn't make any poor decisions. He didn't put the ball into coverage anywhere, did a nice job of executing what we wanted him to do. It created balance in our offense, which was really, really good."

Despite that, Saban still wasn't ready to name Coker his full-time starter.

Meanwhile, with Henry not having to take more of a pounding his coaches were able to get

Breaking away from the Badgers' defense, Derrick Henry scores the first touchdown of the game on a 37-yard run.

NOTABLE

Senior Jake Coker was just the fifth player since 2007 to start a game at quarterback for the Crimson Tide, joining John Parker Wilson, Greg McElroy, AJ McCarron and Blake Sims. Of the four who were making their first career start Coker had the best passer efficiency rating of 172.3.

other players some needed work. Among them was senior running back Kenyan Drake, who was playing in his first game since sustaining a horrific leg fracture at Ole Miss in 2014.

He had a confidence-building 77 rushing yards on 10 carries, and on third-and-26 kept the play alive with a spin move out of a tackle and turned it into a 43-yard touchdown.

Coming in a lot was made of the running back matchup, with Corey Clement having a career 7.0 average per carry and Wisconsin's top running back having topped 1,600 rushing yards in each of the past four seasons.

However, Clement never got going. Limited by a groin injury he managed just 16 rushing yards on eight carries, and reserves Taiwan Deal and Dare Ogunbowale combined for 14 carries for 30 yards. Wide receiver Alex Erickson had the longest run on an end-around for 25 yards, and scored Wisconsin's only touchdown on a 6-yard reception.

Overall, Alabama outgained the Badgers on the ground 238-40, and in total yards 502-268. It could have been a lot more lopsided had the Crimson Tide wanted to pad Henry's numbers.

"He usually plays better as the game goes on in terms of workhorse-type guy," Saban said. ∎

Alabama QBs in First Career Start Since 2007

Name	Opponent	C-A-I	Per.	Yards	TD	Rating
Jake Coker	Wisconsin	15-21-0	71.4	213	1	172.3
Blake Sims	West Virginia	24-33-1	72.7	250	0	130.3
AJ McCarron	Kent State	14-23-2	60.1	226	1	140.4
Greg McElroy	Virginia Tech	15-30-1	50.0	230	1	118.7

Alabama defenders take down Wisconsin running back Taiwan Deal in the first half. The Crimson Tide limited the Badgers to just 40 rushing yards.

ALABAMA 37, MIDDLE TENNESSEE STATE 10
September 12, 2015 • Tuscaloosa, Alabama

OUT OF SYNC
Despite Lopsided Win, Tide Struggles to Find Identity

Looks can sometimes be deceiving, as are scoreboards, like the one that read 37-10 at the end of Alabama's victory in its home opener against Middle Tennessee.

Despite the lopsided outcome, the Crimson Tide didn't play particularly well. The offense didn't click, the defense didn't dominate like it had hoped, and special teams continued to have problems.

That made the subsequent weeks arguably the most important ones of the season, and not just because the next opponent happened to be the team that beat Alabama during the 2014 regular season. Revenge was going to be a factor no matter when Ole Miss visited Bryant-Denny Stadium.

But despite being 2-0 Alabama knew that it needed to find its offensive identity, and fast.

Offensively, the coaching staff needed to figure out which scheme it was going to feature, the pro-style one headed by senior quarterback Jake Coker, or the zone-read that it executed the previously year with Blake Sims, and was obviously better suited for sophomore Cooper Bateman.

Both played a half against the Blue Raiders with less than spectacular results.

"When we play games like this, I told the players that if you don't have the right intensity and the right focus you're going to get exposed," head coach Nick Saban said. "These teams that you play are all good enough to expose you if you don't have the right focus and intensity on what you need to do to go out there and do a good job of finishing. We obviously didn't do a good job getting that point across, because I don't think we finished like we needed to."

It didn't start like it needed to, either.

With Coker playing the first half the offense didn't seem to know if it wanted to establish the pass or the run. He completed 15 of 26 passes for 214 yards, with one touchdown and one interception, but never got into any sort of rhythm.

Some of that had to do with his offensive line and senior Dominick Jackson struggling at right tackle. Even though Coker wasn't sacked he was repeatedly flushed, took numerous hits, and couldn't get comfortable.

Bateman completed 11 of 17 passes for 98 yards in the second half, and like Coker had an interception. While the Bateman's pick was a deep attempt into double coverage giving the Blue Raiders the ball at their own 1 (and eventually led to a blocked punt by Ronnie Harrison for a safety), Bateman's should have been a pick-six.

Defensive back Jeremy Cutrer still returned it 77 yards before he was chased down by freshman running back Damien Harris, and it led to Middle Tennessee's lone touchdown.

⟫⟫⟫ PLAY OF THE GAME

Freshman defensive back Ronnie Harrison blocked a Middle Tennessee punt late in the second quarter for a safety. It was Alabama's first blocked punt since Kenyan Drake notched one against Colorado State on Sept. 21, 2013.

Jonathan Allen (left) and Tim Williams come together to tackle Middle Tennessee quarterback Brent Stockstill during the second half.

"Both guys really need to improve," Saban said about his quarterbacks, who combined to convert just 4 of 13 third-down opportunities.

Meanwhile, Alabama's defense claimed it wanted to be tenacious and relentless, yet was really neither early. Instead it resembled the 2014 unit that was often great in the red zone but otherwise allowed opposing offenses to move the ball.

During the first quarter Alabama was outgained 120-66, and 51-7 on the ground. The Tide did, however, make the first two of four turnovers (three fumble recoveries and an interception).

"I really don't think we got enough," senior linebacker Reggie Ragland said.

It wasn't until a 42-yard play-action pass to junior tight end O.J. Howard in the second quarter that Alabama was able to enjoy any sort of momentum. Although the drive was anything but efficient, junior running back Derrick Henry capped it with a 2-yard touchdown run.

Alabama then started to squeeze the Blue Raiders, who on their following possession converted a third-and-10, but then saw senior cornerback Cyrus Jones pick off the next third-down opportunity. Senior running back Kenyan Drake promptly hit the corner to turn a shovel pass into a 69-yard gain, and Henry walked in a 1-yard touchdown for a 21-3 lead that was the equivalent to a video game screen showing "Game over."

At that point the only questions were how many points would Alabama win by, and how many players would get into the game. The answers were 27 and 66, respectively.

"We played better as the game went on, on defense," Saban said. "They did a lot of things that we weren't very well-prepared for, and we had to make a lot of adjustments during the game, but I thought the players did a really good job of that."

Despite the continuing concerns, like junior kicker Adam Griffith missing two field goals, there were number of things that Alabama coaches don't have to lose sleep over.

Henry finished with 96 rushing yards on 18 carries and scored three more touchdowns, giving him six in two games. Drake continued to be a multi-dimensional force with 202 all-purpose yards and a 14-yard touchdown reception from Bateman.

Alabama also went from 11 penalties a week ago to just five, and got through another game without any significant injuries.

It was also a terrific dress rehearsal for opening Southeastern Conference play against the Rebels and Hugh Freeze's rapid-fire offense. With Alabama's defense getting better and more comfortable as the game progressed the Crimson Tide finished with a 532-275 edge in total yards, and 220-86 in rushing.

But for a team playing what many consider the toughest schedule in the nation and working to instill a take-no-prisoners mentality, things were about to get a lot more difficult.

"We never really seemed like we were in sync, and didn't play like we really wanted to on offense," Saban said. "We made some explosive plays, but there has got to be more consistency and execution." ∎

>>> PLAYER OF THE GAME

Senior running back Kenyan Drake finished with 202 all-purpose yards including 91 receiving, and scored on a 14-yard reception on sophomore quarterback Cooper Bateman's first career touchdown pass.

Derrick Henry runs the ball in for one of his two touchdowns in the second quarter. Henry finished the game with 96 rushing yards on 18 carries.

>>> STATISTIC OF THE GAME:

Alabama's offseason emphasis on creating turnovers looked like it was beginning to pay off. The Crimson Tide forced four for the first time since facing Western Kentucky in 2012.

LINEBACKER

REGGIE RAGLAND

Senior Served as Role Model On and Off the Field

Let there be no doubt, years from now when fans look back at the 2015-16 University of Alabama football team they will say that this was Reggie Ragland's defense.

In addition to improving his overall game, it's what he came back for this final year; that and to try and win another ring.

But even though there were scores of talented players on the Crimson Tide roster and other senior starters on the defense he's the guy to which everyone looked and listened.

"Everybody really counts on him," senior linebacker Dillon Lee said.

Ragland was the primary one to relay the play calls and responsible for the pre-snap adjustments among the front seven. He led that group in tackles for the second straight year and he was one of the few guys remaining who could say that he contributed to crushing Notre Dame in the 2012 national championship game.

Even the offensive players recognized his status.

"He's a great guy," junior wide receiver Chris Black said. "He's definitely a role model for all the younger guys. He sets a great example for the team, on and off the field."

When Nick Saban had to choose who would represent the Crimson Tide during SEC Media Days in July, two of his selections were fairly easy: Ragland and third-year starting center Ryan Kelly (who would be eventually named team captains along with quarterback Jake Coker and running back Derrick Henry). Both embraced that role because they just didn't represent the team, but became spokesmen for the offense and defense.

What Reggie said during that hot July afternoon was definitely heard by his teammates. For example:

Reggie Ragland sacks Spartans quarterback Connor Cook during Alabama's 38-0 shutout of Michigan State in the Cotton Bowl.

"Guys aren't scared to play us any more. Guys come in very happy, excited to play us. I used to see teams break down in the first half and just give up playing, so we've got to get that back.

"We have to get that back."

Ragland was referring to how Alabama was fourth nationally in rushing defense, sixth in scoring defense, No. 12 in total defense, and 30th in pass-efficiency defense during the 2014 season, which at face value was pretty good. However it wasn't by the Crimson Tide's high standards, especially since Alabama was minus two in turnover ratio (turnovers gained minus turnovers lost) and 41st in third-down defense, its worst showing in that statistical category since Saban's first season at the Capstone, 2007.

"Third down is all about will and want-to," Ragland said. "It's all about effort. You just can't get to the quarterback just by going through somebody like that. You have to want to get to the quarterback. You have to do the necessary things."

He also mentioned that some of his teammates had "talked the talk, but didn't walk the walk" when it came to paying attention to detail and putting the team before themselves during the previous postseason. He wasn't necessarily calling anyone out, but sending notice that he was taking ownership of the defense and had the highest expectations.

Make that leader of the defense from a player standpoint. There was no doubt about who really guided the Crimson Tide's pack.

"I felt in the past we had the guys, but it's all about work ethic; a guy's got to want to," Ragland explained. "When you're facing teams like that you have to want to. I think this year we have guys who want to do it. It's all about everyone having the right mindset and I think we're going to get the job done. You've got to run to the ball. You've got to want to do something.

"You don't want to go to school, your mom is going to make you go to school, turn the light on. So you've got to want to go to school so your mom doesn't get on your tail. And that's how it is. That's how Coach Saban is. We've got to do it. You don't want him on your tail,

you've got to want to do it, and after a while and we do it Coach Saban backs off."

Wait, so Saban was like the Crimson Tide's mom?

"I wouldn't say that," Ragland said with a laugh. "Coach Saban is the ruler."

Ragland's comfort in challenging his teammates on a regular basis spoke volumes to how far he had come as a player. Recruited out of Ben Jones High School in Madison, Ala., he was considered a prize in-state prospect but during his first couple of years seemed pretty content with his reserve role on the team.

Granted, he was behind some pretty good interior linebackers like C.J. Mosley and Nico Johnson, but after a couple of years of almost exclusively playing special teams Ragland started to question if he could really play at this level.

That changed in 2014 when he moved into the starting lineup and gave the defense a strong physical presence it hadn't really enjoyed since Rolando McClain and Dont'a Hightower were helping win national championships.

Ragland finished second on the Crimson Tide with 95 tackles, including 10.5 for a loss, which made him a semifinalist for the Butkus Award. He didn't surpass those numbers during his final regular season, in part due to the development of Reuben Foster, which allowed him to line up in some different places including as an occasional pass rusher. Yet he was a unanimous All-American selection and the SEC's Defensive Player of the Year.

"Reggie's a guy who's gotten more and more confident each year," defensive coordinator Kirby Smart said. "He came in very talented. He came in not knowledgeable, not as instinctive as an inside 'backer. He's gotten better every season.

"He practices hard, he plays hard, it's important to Reggie. Reggie wants to please you as a coach. He wants to lead the group as a unit. So he's gotten more confident this year. He'll talk to the freshmen. He'll talk to Reuben. He's making more calls. Maybe he's really a natural leader, but now he has the experience and confidence and accolades to be that guy we need him to be—that bell-cow guy."

Maurice Smith (left) playfully interviews Reggie Ragland (center) and A'Shawn Robinson during media day before the Cotton Bowl.

So when Reggie said something or heaped praise on his teammates it really carried weight, like how the defensive line was looking so good during the spring that he was getting frustrated by how they frequently beat him to the ball carrier. He called Foster a "monster" (in a good way) and freshman defensive tackle Daron Payne a "man-child" before he even took a snap in a game.

"I think one of the things that sometimes gets overlooked is when guys don't play the same position when they come here as what they played in high school, it takes them a little bit more time to develop," Saban said. "Reggie was more of an outside backer/defensive end type guy in high school and moved to inside backer. Each year he's gotten better and better, and now he's one of the most effective players or ranks up there with the most effective players we've ever had here.

"He's certainly taking a responsibility to be more assertive and be more of a leader, which I think is really, really important to the team's success." ■

OLE MISS 43, ALABAMA 37
September 19, 2015 • Tuscaloosa, Alabama

GIVEAWAY

Rebels Score 24 Points Off Turnovers, Upset Tide for Second Straight Season

Head coach Nick Saban called it "disappointing." Senior defensive lineman Jarran Reed said it "hurt." Senior center Ryan Kelly went so far as to use the word "suck" when talking about his team's numerous mistakes.

But the University of Alabama knew it only had to look in the mirror for the primary causes of the 43-37 loss to Ole Miss.

"I don't know anyone we could beat if we're going to give away 31 points," Saban said.

Even though the chances of running the table in the Southeastern Conference were almost none considering the No. 2 Crimson Tide's schedule, this revenge game was supposed to be the one it was most hungry—if not desperate—to win.

Instead, four of Alabama's five turnovers were converted into 24 points and a key breakdown handed the No. 15 Rebels another touchdown in an all-too-familiar way.

Early in the fourth quarter after Alabama had pulled to within 30-24, Ole Miss called for a pop pass very similar to the one that was the difference in the 2013 Iron Bowl—complete with an uncalled penalty for a lineman illegally downfield that was obvious.

"There's a bunch of ups and downs in this game," senior wide receiver Richard Mullaney said after scoring his first two touchdowns with the Crimson Tide. "Even when we were down 19 we still felt like we were in the game."

But the miscues set the tone at the start, with sophomore ArDarius Stewart fumbling the opening kickoff in a manner that was reminiscent of last year's upset, when the Rebels scored the game-winning touchdown off a fumbled return. This time the result was just a 32-yard field goal.

But a Trae Elston interception of a deep ball thrown by quarterback Cooper Bateman, who made the surprising start, put Ole Miss back in Alabama territory—with the quarterback getting blindsided by linebacker Denzel Nkemdiche on the return.

That led to seven points on a fourth-and-goal, when the defense sold out on stopping the run up the middle and running back Jordan Wilkins walked the ball into the end zone following the handoff.

A third turnover, this one the result of a Kenyan Drake fumble on a kick return, set up yet another Ole Miss touchdown, with quarterback Chad Kelly running in from four yards out for a 17-3 lead.

That was the hole Alabama had to try to dig itself out of the rest of the game, only to be further buried by two plays in particular.

The first was about as unusual as they come. After a botched snap, Kelly threw the ball up for standout

⟩⟩⟩ PLAYER OF THE GAME

Both junior running back Derrick Henry and senior linebacker Reggie Ragland did their part, leading the Crimson Tide with 127 rushing yards and nine tackles, respectively.

Running back Kenyan Drake is brought down by Mississippi defensive back Kailo Moore during the second half. For the second season in a row, Alabama suffered its first loss at the hands of Ole Miss.

wide receiver Laquon Treadwell to avoid a sack only to see it deflect off a helmet. It ended up in the hands of teammate Quincy Adeboyejo, who caught it in stride with no one between the wide receiver and the end zone. The "fluke," as Saban referred to it, ended up being a 66-yard touchdown.

The other was the 73-yard score on the pop pass, which was initially flagged as an illegal pass but overturned by replay.

"Oh, man, what a game," said Ole Miss' Hugh Freeze, the first SEC head coach to beat Saban twice in a row since Les Miles in 2010-11. "It was definitely a four-quarter battle. We thought we had it put away a couple of times and they just wouldn't go away."

Although Ole Miss converted only four of 14 third-down opportunities, compared to 11 of 20 for Alabama, Kelly completed 18 of 33 passes for 341 yards, three touchdowns and no interceptions, while rushing eight times for 21 yards and another score. Aided by the pop pass, Cody Core had four receptions for 123 yards.

At times, Alabama showed flashes of its potential, but also ineptitude. Among the positives, the defensive front seven led numerous big stops. Senior quarterback Jake Coker came off the bench to pass for 201 yards and three touchdowns, junior running back Derrick Henry had 127 rushing yards on 23 carries and one touchdown, and Alabama compiled 503 yards of total offense.

But Alabama's final possession ended up being typical of the night. The Crimson Tide had a first down with 31 seconds remaining and went, in order, incomplete (out of bounds), incomplete (deflected), incomplete (drop), and incomplete (high pass). Alabama didn't even get a Hail Mary attempt off into the end zone.

Crimson Tide fans weren't used to this sort of outcome. Alabama had been 25-1 in the series as the home team (including 12 straight wins) and 47–10–2 overall. Saban was 12-1 in SEC home openers, and the team hadn't lost in September since 2007 (29-0).

Although Alabama fell to Ole Miss in 2014, and Rebels fans responded by storming the field, the Crimson Tide still managed to win the SEC title. With this loss coming a month earlier in the schedule it would make repeating only that much tougher as Ole Miss (3-0, 1-0) and LSU had the inside track after having notched key SEC West wins, and Texas A&M had also yet to lose.

It all made Alabama's game at Georgia two weeks later loom larger. It would either be the launching point for the rest of the season or the beginning of a very long and grueling grind.

"We are disappointed; we lost," junior defensive end Jonathan Allen said. "This was a giveaway win. This loss is on us."

"We just have a lot of things we have to do better," Saban said. ◼

⟫⟫ PLAY OF THE GAME

On his nine-yard touchdown to pull Alabama to within 17-10, senior wide receiver Richard Mullaney hurdled a defender en route to the end zone. "I really wasn't thinking, just out there playing football. I just wanted to get in the end zone," said Mullaney, who finished the game with seven receptions for 61 yards and two touchdowns.

⟫⟫ NOTABLE:

The loss snapped Alabama's 29-game winning streak in the month of September, and the Crimson Tide had won 17 straight at home which had tied Baylor for the longest active streak in the Football Bowl Subdivision. It was also the first time in series history that Alabama lost two straight to Ole Miss.

Richard Mullaney hurdles Mississippi's Kendarius Webster to score on a nine-yard reception in the second quarter.

ALABAMA 34, LOUISIANA-MONROE 0
September 26, 2015 • Tuscaloosa, Alabama

DEFENSIVE DOMINANCE

Ragland, Crimson Tide Limit ULM to 92 Yards in Shutout

All week long, Alabama senior linebacker Reggie Ragland was talking to his teammates. His message was simple and one the Crimson Tide obviously took to heart.

"Reggie Ragland kept saying: 'No one's scoring on us,'" senior safety Geno Matias-Smith said. "That's kind of been our motto."

Alabama's defense subsequently did exactly what its leader said. It was the game the coaches had been looking for in terms of swarming to the ball, being relentless, and affecting the quarterbacks. Alabama did all that and more while shutting out Louisiana-Monroe 34-0.

Against an opponent that had been averaging 30.5 points and 422.0 yards per game, which included the season-opening matchup against Southeastern Conference foe Georgia, Alabama's defensive numbers were pretty staggering.

The Crimson Tide allowed just 92 total yards, including just nine rushing, while tallying six sacks and 12 tackles for a loss, two interceptions, eight passes broken up, and eight hurries.

It appeared at times that the No. 12 Crimson Tide was simply taking turns with the brutal hits and big stops, while the Warhawks' biggest offensive play was just 10 yards.

"We were playing physical and attacked, we dominated the line of scrimmage," senior defensive lineman Jarran Reed said, while noting that the Crimson Tide hardly blitzed.

Considering Alabama's upcoming schedule—with SEC foes Arkansas, Tennessee, and Texas A&M following Georgia in the month of October alone—the defense's timing couldn't have been better. More than notching Alabama's 15th shutout since Nick Saban took over as head coach in 2007, through four games the Crimson Tide had yielded only 227 rushing yards on 115 attempts.

That's an average of 1.97 yards per carry.

"We played with a lot of toughness, especially on defense," Saban said.

While Alabama's offense didn't grind out yards like its first three games, part of that had to do with some vanilla play-calling and also having a limited backfield.

With junior Derrick Henry not practicing much during the week due to tonsillitis, he only had 13 carries for 52 yards. Saban indicated that senior Kenyan Drake had sustained a minor injury against Ole Miss and had just 10 carries for 65 yards.

With freshman Bo Scarbrough serving the last game of his four-game eligibility suspension, true freshman Damien Harris became a bigger part of the rotation, and even played during in the first quarter.

Meanwhile, the passing game took some time to get going as Alabama converted only two of its first nine

>>> PLAY OF THE GAME

Players who join the Crimson Tide as a walk-on don't get too many chances to score, so when tight end Michael Nysewander caught a 19-yard touchdown pass the Alabama bench celebrated like it had just scored against Auburn.

Alabama defenders take down Louisiana-Monroe running back Kaylon Watson in the first half. The Crimson Tide defense held the Warhawks to 92 total yards, including just nine rushing yards.

third-down opportunities and had four dropped passes in the first half.

Its lone turnover was pretty horrendous as well, as senior quarterback Jake Coker was hit as he threw, resulting in a deep wounded duck that safety Tre' Hunter caught at midfield.

"I have to be more conservative when it comes to taking shots, especially in traffic when I'm trying to get the ball out," said Coker, who completed 17 of 31 passes for 158 yards and three touchdowns. "I can't do the things I've been doing."

But in the second half the offense got into a better rhythm even though offensive coordinator Lane Kiffin was obviously trying to get the reserves more involved. Former walk-on Michael Nysewander scored a rare touchdown on a 19-yard reception, which tied for the longest completion of the game, and sophomore wide receiver ArDarius Stewart had a 16-yard score off an impressive bootleg.

"Occasionally they'll toss the rock out there to me," said Nysewander, who speculated that it made his mother the happiest person at Bryant-Denny Stadium. "After (taking) sort of a gut-punch last week after the way we fought, and (coming) up on the losing end, it was nice to get that team win today."

Nevertheless, despite some of the offensive shortcomings for the first time this season Alabama really looked like Alabama.

During the previous week's loss to Ole Miss it gave up 433 total yards, of which 139 came on two very unusual plays. Otherwise, the Rebels' longest drive was just 51 yards.

ULM (1-2) would have loved to have one go that far. Its best was just 31 yards. The first six possessions resulted in minus-13 rushing yards and nine total yards, for an average of .5 yards per snap. It didn't have a first down until executing a fake punt at its own 20-yard line.

Quarterback Garrett Smith was 17 of 37 for 74 yards with two interceptions, and leading wide receiver Ajalen Holley made nine receptions, but for just 38 yards.

"Alabama's defense is a lot bigger," ULM wide receiver Ajalen Holley said in comparing the Crimson Tide to the Bulldogs. "Georgia's defense is a lot faster. That's as good as I can give you right there. They're both sound defenses. They're really good defenses.

"When it comes to running the ball, I feel like we could be on the edge a little better against Alabama. When it comes to Georgia, we couldn't, because they're a faster outside defense. When it comes to getting downhill, I feel like Alabama is better at filling the gap than Georgia is because they're bigger. Their defensive line can fill gaps better than Georgia. That's from my perspective."

Nevertheless, the Warhawks had a lot more success against the Bulldogs and scored two touchdowns.

"Alabama is a little bit more versatile, as in the pass game is outside of the box," Hunter said. "Georgia is light inside of the box. Alabama can spread you out. Playing in space is always hard. For skilled guys and linemen, playing in space is always hard. There is a bit more to think about than gearing up for box plays."

But even though it might be tabbed the underdog for the first time in a long time, Alabama would go into its showdown at Sanford Stadium having reclaimed some of its swagger, which was extremely important.

"We got a lot better," Matias-Smith said. "The biggest thing was execution." ■

⟫⟫⟫ PLAYER OF THE GAME

The whole defense could share the honor, but senior defensive lineman Jarran Reed was credited with five tackles including two for a loss and one sack, a broken-up pass, and a quarterback hurry during his rotation time.

Senior Michael Nysewander, a former walk-on, scores on a 19-yard pass from Jake Coker in the third quarter.

>>> **STATISTIC OF THE GAME:**

ULM had just 92 yards of total offense, averaging 1.2 yards per play. Its most successful drive lasted 11 plays for 30 yards and the Warhawks punted 12 times.

QUARTERBACK

JAKE COKER

Signal Caller Stepped Up Game to Quiet Critics

There were a lot of messages being sent throughout the University of Alabama football complex during the days following the loss to Ole Miss.

There was head coach Nick Saban having senior quarterback Jake Coker take all of the first-team reps in practices, which he had never done before.

There was a players-only meeting during which the talk centered on everyone ignoring what was being said outside of the locker room and what senior center Ryan Kelly called "negative noise."

There was also what senior running back Derrick Henry said to Coker after the interception in the second quarter of the following victory against Louisiana-Monroe: Don't press.

"[I told him to] keep his head in the game," Henry said. "There was a lot of game left to play, just go out and make plays and don't let it affect him."

It was good advice, which will likely be repeated before the subsequent showdown at No. 8 Georgia, where No. 13 Alabama was an underdog for the first time since the 2009 SEC Championship Game against Tim Tebow and Florida. It had fans wondering if Coker could win such a big game "Between the Hedges" at Sanford Stadium.

All they had to go on were his first four games, especially his ULM performance that was viewed as sort of a mixed bag. While the defense played lights out, the offense didn't quite execute as some had hoped, and Alabama didn't pound the ball as expected.

That was partly because of the primary running backs being limited, so Alabama focused on working through some things in the passing game during Coker's debut as the full-time starting quarterback.

"Eventually, I got things going and finished the way I wanted to finish," he said. "I thought I got better, but at the same time, I had some mistakes. There were guys in the wrong position and it was my fault. I have a long way to go."

Jake Coker releases a long pass during Alabama's win over Michigan State in the Cotton Bowl. Coker completed 25 of 30 passes in the win.

There's no doubt, though, that Coker played better and looked more comfortable as the game progressed. Specifically, after completing 10 of 21 passes for 80 yards in the first half the graduate transfer from Florida State was 7 of 10 for 78 yards before being pulled in the second half.

One of his last incompletions was the dropped pass that should have been a touchdown by freshman wide receiver Calvin Ridley, and Coker also didn't get credit for a 13-yard pass to sophomore ArDarius Stewart when sophomore left tackle Cam Robinson was flagged for being illegally downfield (although replay clearly showed that he wasn't past the three-yard limit).

Alabama did a lot of crossing and slant routes and numerous times essentially ran the same plays over and over again with varying personnel or with what Saban likes to call different "window dressing."

"We played it pretty tight to the vest today, and I think we probably need to do a little more," Saban said after the game. "I thought Jake did a good job, and however you look at the stops, you've got to look at the drops. That wasn't really his fault; he made some good throws. There was probably a couple times that he wishes he would have done it a little different, in terms of going to somebody else, and those are the things we need to work out and get better at."

After reviewing the game film, Saban said there were six dropped passes. Stewart, junior Chris Black, sophomore Cam Sims and Ridley all had an obvious one, but part of the game plan was to get more players involved.

"We do take it to heart," Stewart said about the drops.

Still, when Coker talked about improving, he was mostly referring to things like not going through his progression and locking in on one receiver. A perfect example was a pass intended for O.J. Howard against Ole Miss that was picked off. Coker never took his eyes off the junior tight end.

On the ULM interception, Henry had just slipped out into open field and had Coker noticed him it could have resulted in a big gain. On third-and-3, he tried to force a pass to Ridley for an incompletion. Senior wide receiver Richard Mullaney was open on a crossing route.

That's normal, though, and part of the learning process.

Alabama's offense, with nine new starters, also had trouble with the blitz, which Georgia has surely noticed, but one thing Coker didn't attempt in the second half was another deep pass, which could only be taken as a sign of improvement. Despite his obvious arm strength he had yet to connect on a home run ball, while the receivers hadn't gotten separation or gone up to try to make a play … yet.

"Obviously, we've got some young receivers out there playing who have not played much that need to develop more confidence," Saban said. "I think Calvin Ridley is playing well and I think ArDarius Stewart can be a really good player for us. We've just got to get a little more consistent with what we're doing, and we've got to bring some of the young guys along. Richard has done a good job all year long."

The key word there was confidence, which only develops through repetition and experience, yet there were two important things to keep in mind regarding the looming challenge in Athens:

1) Coker was the one to lead Alabama in its comeback back against Ole Miss, which, like Georgia, has a very good defense.

2) If everything went the way Alabama hoped he won't have to try to lead the team to wins. Although Saban wanted the offense to be as balanced as possible, the Crimson Tide's trademarks remained a powerful running back and imposing defense.

The coach never wanted to have to put the game in the quarterback's hands unless he had to.

"The more games that he starts, the more reps that he gets, the confidence level is only going to go up, and I think people are starting to notice that," Kelly summarized. "If I know Jake, I know he's going to be the most well-prepared that he can. The guy studies his (rear) off, and I just know that's what he's going to do. He's going to give us the best chance to win." ■

Jake Coker laughs during a Jan. 6, 2016 press conference in Tuscaloosa. Coker transferred to Alabama in 2014 and backed up Blake Sims in 2014 before emerging as the starting quarterback in 2015.

EXTRAORDINARY

Crimson Tide Manhandle No. 8 Bulldogs in Statement Victory

Apparently there's nothing like a trip to Sanford Stadium to fix whatever ails the Alabama football team.

Similar to the famous blackout game of 2008, when it first served noticed to what college football could expect with Nick Saban heading the Crimson Tide, Alabama again dominated the preseason favorite in the SEC East on its home field, this time with a 38-10 result.

Like that previous meeting, which ended up 41-30 in favor of Alabama after it led 31-0 at halftime, the score and statistics weren't indicative of how lopsided the game truly was. It simply manhandled No. 8 Georgia in the rain.

No. 13 Alabama (4-1 overall, 1-1 SEC) shook off the growing pains of the season's first month and played with poise, dominated both lines of scrimmage, and again played relentless defense. With some of its younger players beginning to come into their own it again looked like a strong contender for both the SEC championship and playoffs.

"I was really proud of our players today, our team today," Saban said. "I thought this was a difficult challenge for them. I told them before the game that the plan that we had for them ordinary men couldn't go out there and get it done. We needed them to be extraordinary and that they were, and they were special."

Although the hyped Derrick Henry vs. Nick Chubb showdown essentially ended up being a statistical draw, 148 yards to 146, Chubb turned out to be the only bright spot for the Bulldogs (4-1, 2-1 SEC). After being shut down until there were 19 seconds remaining in the third quarter he took advantage of a botched formation that left a key open gap for his 83-yard touchdown.

With it Chubb notched his 13th straight 100-yard rushing game to break Herschel Walker's team record. Of course Alabama was up by five touchdowns at the time, but it still bothered Saban afterward.

"I thought we played great defensively minus the one play," he said.

"We can't let anybody get anything," senior defensive lineman Jarran Reed said.

Seven of Georgia's nine possessions during the first half were three-and-out, and it couldn't even take advantage of a Henry fumble in Alabama territory. With Chubb having 10 carries for 39 yards and quarterback Greyson Lambert on the bench after completing just 7 of 17 passes for 70 yards the average gain per snap was 9.1 for the Crimson Tide and 3.6 for the Bulldogs.

Meanwhile, Alabama found the end zone in three very different ways during the second quarter.

The first was Henry's 30-yard touchdown run that was reminiscent of the season opener against Wisconsin

⟩⟩⟩ PLAY OF THE GAME

Junior safety Eddie Jackson's 50-yard interception return and freshman Minkah Fitzpatrick's blocked punt return scored more points than the entire Georgia team.

Jake Coker throws as pass in the first half of Alabama's win over No. 8 Georgia. Coker completed 11 of 16 passes for 190 yards.

when he turned a hole on the left side into six points.

The second was a blocked punt in which freshman Minkah Fitzpatrick completely smothered the ball coming off Collin Barber's foot and made it look easy. He was credited with 1-yard return for the demoralizing touchdown.

Finally, senior quarterback Jake Coker got into the mix by finally connecting on a deep ball, with a 45-yard strike to Calvin Ridley that had offensive coordinator Lane Kiffin doing a celebratory arm-pump on the sideline. The two also had a 50-yard completion as the freshman wide receiver had a breakout game and finished with five catches for 120 yards.

"We had a lot of fun out there," said Coker, who completed 11 of 16 passes for 190 yards and wasn't sacked.

Any lingering hope that Georgia still had at halftime quickly vanished on the Bulldogs' first play after the break when junior safety Eddie Jackson picked replacement Brice Ramsey off at midfield and returned it 50 yards for a touchdown.

"We did a pretty good of disguising in the secondary," the converted cornerback said as Alabama had three interceptions and broke up seven more attempts. "We put good pressure on them and tried to make them make mistakes."

Not only did it make the score 31-3, but combined

with the downpour from the remnants of Hurricane Joaquin the touchdown sparked the exodus of soaked fans. Unlike the 2008 game, when Georgia tried to fight back in the second half, this time the Bulldogs just had the one play.

"The dam broke and unfortunately we just didn't have enough counterpunches to get back in it," said Georgia coach Mark Richt, who then used the same line from the 2008 defeat: "We got whipped."

The loss also came after the Georgia players got in the faces of their Alabama counterparts when they were jumping around after coming out of their tunnel to warm up, and later taunted them from midfield. Saban admitted that he was "really pissed" about his team's initial focus, but the Crimson Tide then simply went about its business and saved everything else for the game.

"Everyone calmed down and we played really good ball," senior linebacker Reggie Ragland said. "You don't want to get too hyped up in warm-ups, you want to be able to play hard to the end. You have to stay calm and be cool."

Alabama was also motivated by being called an underdog, and critics claiming that the Crimson Tide wouldn't be a factor in the chase for the conference title after the loss to Ole Miss.

"We didn't really like it," Coker said. "It's not something we're comfortable with."

This was Alabama's answer.

"I know they've been criticized a lot but I thought we played an outstanding game today," Saban said.

"They believe in this team and I believe in this team." ■

>>> PLAYER OF THE GAME

Running back Derrick Henry and wide receiver Calvin Ridley both reached the century mark while posting career marks. Henry's 146 rushing yards came on a career-high 26 carries, and Ridley's 120 receiving yards made him the first freshman to have a 100-yard receiving game since Amari Cooper in the 2013 BCS National Championship Game.

Freshman wide receiver Calvin Ridley had a breakout game against the Bulldogs, finishing with five catches for 120 yards.

>>> STATISTIC OF THE GAME:

Thanks in part to having the ball for 11 minutes and 8 seconds in the fourth quarter, Alabama dominated time of possession (34:03-25:57). Outside of a 14-play, 71-yard drive that resulted in a first-quarter field goal, Georgia's longest possession lasted just 1:43.

ALABAMA 27, ARKANSAS 14
October 10, 2015 • Tuscaloosa, Alabama

ONE BIG BREAK

Crimson Tide Overcomes Slow Start to Top Razorbacks

There was a moment during the game when it felt like Alabama's season may have been hanging in the balance and it had nothing to do with the scoreboard.

It was early in the second quarter when senior linebacker Reggie Ragland was on the ground grabbing at his left shoulder, which hadn't been the one previously bothering him. Due to a painful stinger he briefly came out, only to return for the next series and drill Jeremy Sprinkle after the tight end made a first-down reception in the flat for no gain.

The message was clear: It's going to take a whole lot to slow down or stop the No. 8 Crimson Tide (5-1, 2-1 Southeastern Conference), especially with its defense prompting descriptions like tenacious, relentless, and dominating.

"We have a strong physical team and any time we face a team like that we have to play grown-man physical football," Ragland said after Alabama celebrated homecoming with a 27-14 victory over Arkansas at Bryant-Denny Stadium. "Our team did that."

With the midway point of the regular season having arrived Alabama has found different ways to be successful, but any discussion about its chances of making a run at the SEC title clearly began and ended with the defense.

Coming off the impressive 38-10 victory at Georgia it didn't have a letdown against an opponent it had trouble with the year before. Although Arkansas running back Alex Collins came in with 656 rushing yards, and averaged 131.2 per game, his longest carry was just 5 yards en route to 12 carries for 26 yards.

Senior quarterback Brandon Allen had a little more success, but not much, and 54 of his 176 passing yards came on one play after the outcome was no longer in doubt and Alabama had started inserting reserves.

"Offensively the story of the day was that we just couldn't do anything with any consistency," Arkansas head coach Bret Bielema said. "We couldn't run it, couldn't throw it, and couldn't convert the first downs the way we needed to.

"One thing about Alabama, their defense is unique to them."

While the Crimson Tide's defensive depth might have be unparalleled, especially on the line, and the young secondary was making strides each game, doing whatever it took to have everyone playing well together was Ragland's primary job—and it's a responsibility he more than embraced.

That's what Ragland meant to the defense, and what the defense meant to the Crimson Tide's outlook.

"This is when you find out who you are, and how

⟫⟫⟫ PLAY OF THE GAME

Freshman Calvin Ridley's 81-yard touchdown reception was the 11th longest in Alabama history. It was also the turning point of the game as it sparked a 24-point rally by the Crimson Tide.

Arkansas running back Alex Collins tries unsuccessfully to break through Alabama's defensive front. The Crimson Tide limited the Razorbacks to just 44 yards on the ground.

bad you do what you want to do," Coach Nick Saban said.

"Reggie played a really good game tonight, he had a lot of tackles, knocked down a couple of balls and was really a good leader out there. Reggie's played well for us all year and this was probably one of his best games."

Although Ragland said he thought he did "all right. I'm my worst critic." He was credited with a team-high eight tackles, a forced fumble a pass broken up and two quarterback hurries.

Overall, the defense tallied three sacks, four tackles for a loss, two turnovers, six passes broken up and nine quarterback hurries.

"I thought we had a really good game," senior defensive lineman Jarran Reed said. "I thought we executed well again, and we played well as a defensive unit."

The first half was almost all Crimson Tide, which drove 80 yards on its first possession and 60 on its second, but only had three points to show for them.

With senior quarterback Jacob Coker taking a hard hit as he threw a deep ball to tight end O.J. Howard the pass was picked off by Josh Liddell, and two possessions later an attempt to senior wide receiver Richard Mullaney was deflected and caught by Santos Ramirez.

It was Alabama's ninth turnover in SEC play, compared to just four takeaways (all against Georgia in the rain).

The first time the Razorbacks (2-4, 1-2 SEC) had the ball in Crimson Tide territory, at the 12-yard line after Ramirez's return and an unsportsmanlike penalty on left tackle Cam Robinson, they scored on a play-action crossing route by wide receiver Drew Morgan for a 4-yard touchdown.

Despite having just 77 yards of total offense Arkansas actually led 7-3 at halftime.

However, the prevailing feeling at Bryant-Denny Stadium was that if Alabama could get one break, one big play to give it the momentum, the result would be like watching a crack on a windshield get quickly out of control.

The fissure began on first down at the Alabama 19 when Coker connected on a long pass to freshman Calvin Ridley for an 81-yard touchdown.

It not only sent Bryant-Denny Stadium into a frenzy but also caused Arkansas to make a desperate decision that backfired. After going three-and-out punter Toby Baker took off on fourth-and-5 only to get stopped short of the first down by freshman Shawn Burgess-Becker.

Alabama quickly drove and scored on a 3-yard touchdown catch by Mullaney, followed by a 35-yard field goal by junior kicker Adam Griffith that was set up by an Eddie Jackson interception, and junior running back Derrick Henry's 1-yard touchdown plunge.

Until the late score, a 54-yard touchdown by wide receiver Dominque Reed with just 1 minute, 37 seconds remaining, the Razorbacks' longest drive was just 26 yards.

"All in all, I thought our defense played extremely well," Saban said, and no one was going to argue the point.

Unlike last year when Alabama continually attacked Allen with five or six players, this time it went with more of a base approach by continually rotated everyone in the front seven and the Razorbacks were still overmatched. It would have to go with a very different approach, with more nickel and dime packages a week later at Texas A&M, where the Aggies had the advantage of being rested from a bye week.

"You have to be in shape to run all over the place," Ragland said about stopping the Razorbacks. "Next week I really have to be in shape." ■

>>> PLAYER OF THE GAME

Senior linebacker Reggie Ragland had a performance that the numbers didn't adequately reflect even though he led the Crimson Tide with eight tackles (seven solo), a sack, two quarterback hurries, and a forced fumble.

Derrick Henry flies downfield against Arkansas. Henry ran for 95 yards, including a 1-yard touchdown run in the fourth quarter.

SECONDARY TO NONE

Defensive Backs Stepped Up Their Game in 2015

Even though the game was a turning point in the career of Cyrus Jones, it was a rough afternoon for the University of Alabama cornerback.

Two years ago at Texas A&M, Jones was thrown into the fire, which in this case was an accurate description because of the brutal heat on September 14th and Mike Evans.

After the talented wide receiver and Johnny Manziel started to light up the Crimson Tide secondary, Jones was inserted, and then swapped spots with cornerback Deion Belue to try and slow them down.

Alabama survived, 49-42, but gave up a program-record 628 total yards while Manziel and Evans set Texas A&M marks with 464 passing yards and 279 receiving.

"I grew up a lot that day, let's just put it that way," Jones said. "It was just a great game, back and forth. That was my first time really being out there in that type of atmosphere. It was definitely a learning experience."

It should also be noted that Jones also made the play of the game when he reacted to Manziel's overthrow of a fade into the end zone for a crucial interception. Even Nick Saban called it a "huge play" after saying that Evans "had his way with our corners pretty much all day."

"That was cool," Jones said of the pick.

Granted, he went to on become essentially a shutdown defensive back in the Southeastern Conference, but Alabama's use of a converted wide receiver (Jones) and a junior-college transfer (Belue) at cornerback was reflective of the problems it had at the position.

Alabama had been known for its standout corners, with Kareem Jackson (2010), Dee Kirkpatrick (2012),

and Dee Milliner (2013) all first-round draft selections after leaving early. It also had Ha Ha Clinton-Dix and Landon Collins at safety, but it took until 2015 for the secondary to really get back to its high standard of play.

Thanks to a recruiting bonanza that was sparked by 5-star prospects Tony Brown and Marlon Humphrey, whom were regarded as two of the top three cornerbacks in the nation in the Class of 2014, Alabama again had depth in the secondary—so much that a 5-star cornerback (Kendall Sheffield) and a 4-star safety (Deionte Thompson) redshirted in 2015.

"I think we have a lot of weapons in our secondary this year that we probably didn't (have the last two years)," junior tight end O.J. Howard said. "A lot of guys rotate in. A lot of guys are fresh."

Even though there were often three freshmen in the dime package when it used six defensive backs, by the midway point of the season newcomers like Minkah Fitzpatrick and Ronnie Harrison had already made some big plays.

Fitzpatrick, a starter in the nickel package, was tied for the team lead in passes broken up (six), to go with two sacks and a blocked punt that he recovered for a touchdown at Georgia. Harrison made two interceptions and blocked a punt that resulted in a safety.

"You can definitely see they're growing up, and they're just more confident every time they step out there," Jones said. "I knew it would come with time, just like it did for me. I just think they're progressing gradually."

The key change, though, may have been when junior Eddie Jackson switched from cornerback to

Defensive back Cyrus Jones (center) receives congratulations from teammates after intercepting a Connor Cook pass during the second quarter of Alabama's win over Michigan State in the Cotton Bowl.

replace Collins at strong safety, which at the time was considered a bit of a risk. Combined with senior Geno Matias-Smith landing the free safety job what Alabama gave up in size at the positions it more than made up for in speed and range, which helped against spread, up-tempo offenses.

After the SEC Championship Game, Jackson led the Crimson Tide with five interceptions, returning two for a touchdown, which helped lead to being selected a second-team All-American by both the Walter Camp Foundation and the Football Writers Association of America.

His 40 tackles weren't on the same level as Collins, who led the team in that category in 2014, but Matias-Smith, Fitzpatrick, and Humphrey all had at least that many as well.

"I think he was a little apprehensive at first of the move, only because it was out of his comfort zone and he hadn't done it for a long time," Saban said. "There were a lot of new things he was going to have to learn, but he's been very dedicated in his approach to try and learn the position and do the things at the position that you need to do to play winning football.

"He's always been a very instinctive sort of playmaker guy, even when he played corner. So that's carried right over into safety, and he's done a really good job for us."

In 2014 the perception was that Alabama was succeeding almost in spite of its secondary, only to get exposed at the end of the season.

Consequently, there were three important areas that were especially targeted for improvement, all of which were at least partially tied to the secondary: turnovers, third downs and giving up big plays.

There was obvious progress in the first two categories:

Opponents went from converting 33 percent of their third-down opportunities (27-for-83) to just 28 percent (55-for-197), which before the playoffs ranked sixth in the nation. Moreover, the Crimson Tide was neck-and-neck with Clemson for the national league in defensive three-and-outs.

As for turnovers Alabama had just nine forced fumbles and 10 interceptions in 2014. It had 24 after beating Florida in the 2015 SEC Championship Game with four pickoffs returned for touchdowns.

The occasional big play still occurred, but combined with the with the imposing front seven playing at a higher level the difference in the defense's overall confidence was obvious.

"I feel like we help the linebackers, the linebackers help the DBs and we also look out for the DBs by putting pressure on the quarterback, and they get picks," junior defensive lineman Dalvin Tomlinson said. "So we affect each other on the field in practice and stuff."

That's why after the midseason victory against Arkansas both Jones and Jackson said that they thought Alabama had had the best defense in the nation. Really no one could argue the point.

"Most definitely, we are the best defense in the country, hands down," Jackson said. "We come in every day in practice and use all the critics and things and use it to fuel our fire and come in to work hard."

"As long as we come out there and execute like we're supposed to I don't think anybody can beat us," Jones said. ■

ALABAMA'S SECONDARY SECOND-TO-NONE

Pos.	Name	Year	Recruiting Ranking
CB	Cyrus Jones	Sr.	4 stars-2012, 4th Athlete
	Bradley Sylve	Sr.	4-2011, 15th WR
	Maurice Smith	Jr.	4-2013, 9th CB
CB	Marlon Humphrey	R-Fr.	5-2014, 3rd CB
	Tony Brown	So.	5-2014, 2nd CB
	Minkah Fitzpatrick	Fr.	5-2015, 5th CB
SS	Eddie Jackson	Jr.	3-2013, 14th Athlete
	Ronnie Harrison	Fr.	4-2015, 12th S
	Shawn Burgess-Becker	Fr.	4-2015, 10th Athlete
FS	Geno Matias-Smith	Sr.	4-2012, 4th CB
	Hootie Jones	So.	4-2014, 4th S

Alabama's depth chart and 247Sports

Alabama cornerback Minkah Fitzpatrick brings down Texas A&M receiver Ricky Seals-Jones during the Crimson Tide's win over the Aggies on Oct. 17. Fitzpatrick, a freshman, was a starter in Alabama's nickel package.

ALABAMA 41, TEXAS A&M 23
October 17, 2015 • College Station, Texas

HENRY'S HEISMAN MOMENT?

RB Runs Over Aggies for 236 Yards, 2 TDs

When the University of Alabama completed its 41-23 victory at Texas A&M, everyone who had been at Kyle Field, from former President George H. W. Bush to Houston Astros rookie shortstop Carlos Correa, probably had the same opinion of running back Derrick Henry: "I'm glad I don't have to try and tackle him."

With 32 attempts for 236 yards Henry had a career game despite facing the No. 9 team on its home field, and also scored two more touchdowns.

He'd reached the end zone in 12 straight games, which was not only the longest active streak in the nation, but an Alabama record (previously held by Terry Davis with 10 in 1971-72).

"Derrick Henry had a fabulous game," Nick Saban said during his postgame press conference. "But you have to say something about the offensive line (too).

"He's a workhorse, he's tough."

The rushing yards were the most by an Alabama player since Mark Ingram tallied 246 against South Carolina in 2009, when he all but put the team on his back and kept running out of the wildcat despite everyone in the stadium knowing where he was going over and over again.

Many consider that game Ingram's signature, or Heisman Trophy moment with the Crimson Tide. With LSU's Leonard Fournette overshadowing everyone in college football through the first half of the 2015 season the same couldn't quite be said of Henry, but he was averaging 128.7 yards per game, which put him on pace for 1,544.6 rushing yards during the regular season with one to three games still to play.

The school single-season rushing record was 1,679 yards set by Trent Richardson in 2011. Henry was also in position to take a shot at Richardson's record of 21 rushing touchdowns during that same season.

"He's a man," Texas A&M coach Kevin Sumlin said of Henry during his postgame press conference.

Henry's previous game highs were 148 yards on 26 carries at Georgia earlier in the month. He matched the yardage with his first eight carries in the first quarter, including a 55-yard touchdown run. He then scored again on the first play of the second quarter, this time from 6 yards.

At that point in the game Henry was averaging 15.9 yards per carry and Texas A&M was looking

>>> PLAY OF THE GAME

Junior safety Eddie Jackson's 93-yard interception return for a touchdown gave Alabama a 28-6 lead in the second quarter and proved to be the game-winning points.

Derrick Henry rushed for 236 yards and two touchdowns to lead Alabama over No. 9 Texas A&M.

foolish for trying to stop the Crimson Tide with a nickel package that Alabama gashed with ease.

Combined with junior safety Eddie Jackson's 93-yard interception return for a touchdown, the first of three pick-sixes for Alabama as the defense outscored the Aggies offense, and the Crimson Tide appeared to be in complete control.

Only two major things occurred to keep Texas A&M (5-1 overall, 2-1 SEC) from calling it a day early. First, senior center Ryan Kelly, who opened up the huge hole on Henry's first touchdown, headed to the locker room with concussion symptoms and did not return.

On third-and-15 with 4:12 before halftime he looked a little woozy after taking on charging linebacker A.J. Hilliard, although with the Texas heat it initially didn't appear to be too much out of the ordinary.

Yet that was the first in a string of mishaps for the Crimson Tide, including four on special teams: Christian Kirk's 68-yard punt return for a touchdown, Shaun Dion Hamilton's targeting penalty, Cyrus Jones losing the ball on a punt return, and a blocked punt.

Texas A&M scored a touchdown following the fumble, while the two other gaffes resulted in missed field-goal attempts. Still, Texas A&M was within striking distance at 28-20.

Similarly, with redshirt freshman J.C. Hassenauer filling in at center and Texas A&M aggressively attacking the line of scrimmage, Alabama's four possessions following Kelly's injury resulted in just 16 yards.

"Probably the thing I'm more proud of is when we lost the momentum of the game in the second quarter after we sort of dominated the first quarter, and they

hit the punt return," Saban said. "We didn't have a lot of fire in our eyes at halftime. The players really responded well.

"It was hot, they were tired and they got their second wind."

What got Alabama going again was a six-minute, 13-play drive that stalled in the red zone, but junior kicker Adam Griffith's 32-yard field goal made it a two-score game again and that was all the breathing room the No. 10 Crimson Tide (6-1 overall, 3-1 SEC) needed.

Henry had one of the key plays on the drive when on fourth-and-2, and Saban trying to call time out only to get visually blocked by offensive coordinator Lane Kiffin, he took a flip and with essentially no blockers ahead of him on the left side due to an unbalanced line still went 6 yards for the first down.

"The shot clock was down to one," Saban said. "I'm glad we didn't (call time out)."

Freshman cornerback Minkah Fitzpatrick's second interception return for a touchdown—55 yards after his first was for 33 yards to open the scoring—eventually sealed the win.

"Bottom line, that's a good football team, Alabama," Sumlin said. "But you also can't play the way we did tonight, giving up 21 points, and expect to win the game."

Overall, the Crimson Tide outgained the Aggies 258-32 on the ground, but A&M notched 15 tackles for a loss, most following Kelly's departure and the defensive linemen beating the snap on the silent count.

The good news for Alabama was that Kelly was expected to be fine, and the Crimson Tide only had to play one more game, against visiting Tennessee, before its bye week.

It wasn't clear who would need it more, Henry or the players trying to stop the running back listed as 6-foot-3, 242 pounds. ▪

⟫⟫ PLAYER OF THE GAME

Junior running back Derrick Henry had a new career high for rushing yards by the end of the first quarter en route to 236 yards on 32 carries and two touchdowns.

Aggies quarterback Kyler Murray recovers his own fumble in the third quarter. The Alabama defense forced two fumbles on the day.

ALABAMA 19, TENNESSEE 14
October 24, 2015 • Tuscaloosa, Alabama

FINDING A WAY

Fourth Quarter Heroics Push Tide to
Ninth Consecutive Win Over Vols

They would spend the rest of the night, weekend, and even month mulling over what to name this one, while enjoying the smell of cigar smoke one more time.

Rocky sack?

T-sized turnover?

Smoked again?

More than anything, though, University of Alabama fans called the 19-14 victory in the "Third Saturday in October" rivalry just what the Crimson Tide needed to set up what could be another championship run.

Alabama was finding out that it had what it takes to do just that.

"It's a great win for our team," Nick Saban said. "We were tired out there today and we didn't look really quick or fast. We didn't have a lot of energy like we usually do, and I think that's due to playing eight games in a row. The best thing I can say is that you have to really respect a team that finds a way to win and makes plays when they have to make plays."

Although No. 8 Alabama had been trying to downplay its incredibly difficult schedule, October was when things were really stacked against the Crimson Tide.

Few, if any other teams could have survived a month-long run of at No. 8 Georgia, Arkansas, at No. 9 Texas A&M, and Tennessee without a loss. All four of those Southeastern Conference opponents had been ranked in 2015 and the last two were coming off byes when they faced the Crimson Tide.

The two-month grind finally caught up to Alabama, which at 7-1 overall (4-1 SEC) really couldn't afford another setback if it wanted to keep its division, league, and playoff hopes alive. But as previous Crimson Tide teams had discovered the ones that play for championships almost always have to endure a scare, and notch a "find-a-way" win like this.

"It was a tough one," senior linebacker Reggie Ragland said. "It shows what kind of team we have.

"Some people grew up tonight and that's what we needed. We needed a game like that to show what kind of tough team we have."

For the first time during the 2015 campaign an opponent scored a touchdown during the opening quarter when Tennessee receiver Josh Smith caught an 11-yard pass from quarterback Joshua Dobbs to cap a 75-yard dive. Alabama had previously outscored opponents 48-6 during the first 15 minutes.

It was also the fourth straight SEC home game, dating back to 2014, in which Alabama didn't have the lead at halftime.

>>> PLAY OF THE GAME

Junior linebacker Ryan Anderson's sack, with the ball going right to junior defensive lineman A'Shawn Robinson, will be one of those plays that will be revisited every year during the days leading up to the annual "Third Saturday in October" showdown.

Alabama defenders Cyrus Jones (left) and Daron Payne take down Tennessee quarterback Joshua Dobbs in the second quarter.

With the offensive line struggling Tennessee tallied 10 tackles for a loss including five sacks. The defensive backs dropped three interceptions while the Volunteers (3-4, 1-3 SEC) missed the same number of field goals, two from 51 yards and the other from 43.

"I don't like to lose," Saban said. "I like to win however we win, and I'm not really particular about how we win."

The game really came down to two fourth quarter possessions, one by each team with the game on the line, just after Tennessee went 75 yards on four plays and took its first lead in the series since 2011, 14-13 on a 12-yard Jalen Hurd run with 5:49 remaining.

Despite having numerous miscues all day, with Alabama having seven penalties and allowing five sacks, the offense went to work. A clutch leaping grab by sophomore wide receiver ArDarius Stewart beat a blitz, and freshman wideout Calvin Ridley matched it on the other sideline for another key first down.

Although Alabama was trying to run down the clock as much as possible with UT still having all of its time outs remaining, getting a touchdown and not just a field goal was the top priority. Three carries by Henry resulted in the points it coveted on a 14-yard misdirection run for a 19-14 lead.

"Same old Henry," Coker said about the running back who finished with 143 rushing yards on 27 carries and two touchdowns. Meanwhile, the quarterback went 21-for-27 for 247 yards and an interception.

"It means a lot," Coker said. "Wish we could have had a few drives go better earlier, but we did what we needed to do."

>>> PLAYER OF THE GAME

Led by junior running back Derrick Henry, who finished with 143 rushing yards on 28 carries and scored two touchdowns, Alabama had the ball for 9:45 in the third quarter and 11:41 of the fourth.

Following Adam Griffith's kickoff that resulted in a touchback, Tennessee had first down at the 25 with 2:24 to go. It managed to get one first down but a false-start penalty put the Vols in a bad hole that Alabama's pass rushers could exploit.

Junior defensive end Jonathan Allen got the first sack and on second-and-24 a defensive play put the game away when junior linebacker Ryan Anderson got to Dobbs, sending the ball sailing to junior defensive end A'Shawn Robinson for the clinching fumble recovery.

"I saw his stance, it was elongated, so I knew it was going to be a pass," said Anderson, before adding about Robinson's attempt at a touchdown return that was stopped short: "I didn't even see him running. I was so hyped up I took off the other way. I might get in trouble for that."

No one noticed immediately because the Alabama sideline essentially turned into a mosh pit of players jumping around, celebrating their ninth straight win over Tennessee.

"It was pretty incredible," said senior center Ryan Kelly, who had barely practiced while recovering from a concussion. "I can say that I never lost to Tennessee. It's kind of up there with the LSU one from last year—the ones that really test this team. We overcame a lot of adversity today and will keep moving forward.

"We're just super excited about how we finished."

Next up was some badly needed rest and recuperation heading into the final stretch of the regular season, when Alabama had another showdown with No. 5 LSU looming on Nov. 7, followed by road games at Mississippi State and Auburn.

It might have taken that long for the players and coaches to get the taste of their victory cigars—per rivalry tradition—out of their mouths, but Alabama considered that a very good problem to have.

"As soon as Coach stopped talking and broke the huddle the whole locker room was a big cloud of smoke," senior cornerback Cyrus Jones said. "It'll overwhelm you in a hurry." ■

Wide receiver ArDarius Stewart leaps over Tennessee defensive back Justin Martin. Stewart had five catches for 88 yards in the win over the Vols. Stewart's leaping catch in the fourth quarter was a key play in Alabama's final scoring drive.

STOPPING THE RUN

Front Seven Led Nation's Best Defense

There's strength in numbers. That much was obvious when it came to the University of Alabama's defensive line during the 2015 season, but the difference was seen in other ways as well.

For example, junior defensive end Jonathan Allen didn't necessarily have to go around opposing linemen in order to get a shot at a quarterback any more, he could go through them too as numerous Crimson Tide opponents learned the hard way.

Lining up in various spots Allen recorded three of his team's nine sacks against Mississippi State and led an assault by the Crimson Tide's front seven that could only be described as relentless and suffocating.

"Jonathan was a really good in high school on the edge as a pass rush guy," head coach Nick Saban said. "Very, very good. I think he has gotten bigger and developed a lot of strength where now he can rush off the edge. But he's a really, really effective inside rusher because he's gotten bigger and stronger.

"He's got enough pop now to turn speed to power on people as well as enough quickness to get by them. That usually is the combination that makes a really good pass-rusher."

The thing is, Saban could almost say the same thing about a number of other Crimson Tide defenders as Alabama got to quarterbacks like no other team in college football.

After the SEC Championship 16 players had been in on a sack and 24 had contributed to a tackle for a loss, although those numbers only told part of the story.

While Alabama was ranked No. 1 against the run the total of 46 sacks topped the nation, and it wasn't like most of them came when games were out of reach or against sub-par competition. Alabama had already faced 10 teams that had been ranked at some point of the season.

That's why the Crimson Tide was widely believed to have the nation's best defense in 2015.

"I thought that was going to be the strength of our team going in, and every one of those guys has gotten better, which is a tribute to their work ethic but also (defensive line coach) Bo Davis has done a nice job with them," Saban said. "Some of the guys got lighter and are quicker. Some of the guys have developed and been able to play more significant roles. I think the diversity we have in players is very helpful."

Although Allen got a little bigger during the offseason, senior Jarran Reed and consensus All-American A'Shawn Robinson shed a few pounds in hopes of being a little faster. Regardless, few opponents had success moving the ball as the Crimson Tide shut down the running lanes and then went after the quarterbacks.

Although Saban doesn't necessarily equate sacks to success—his position has long been it's more about affecting the quarterback—he's still never going to turn one down. When he was at LSU the Tigers went from just 11 sacks in 2000 to 20, 27, and 44 during the national championship season, and 37 in 2004.

The most sacks by a Saban-coached team was during his final season at Michigan State, 1999, when the Spartans had 60 to go with 119 tackles for a loss.

Alabama defensive linemen Jonathan Allen (right) and A'Shawn Robinson sack Florida quarterback Treon Harris during the SEC Championship Game. The Crimson Tide sacked Harris five times in their 29-15 win over the Gators.

Alabama had that same number in 1988 when Derrick Thomas recorded an amazing 27.

Three obvious qualities that stood out about the 2015 front seven were experience, talent, and depth. All the players involved, except for freshman defensive tackle Daron Payne, who quietly started two games, had been in the system for a couple of years and senior linebacker Reggie Ragland led them on the field.

The talent alone was unparalleled, as all the contributors were four- or five-star recruits and the envy of every coach in the nation. Yet the depth was even more impressive. Alabama legitimately rotated nine or 10 defensive linemen, depending on the opponent, who may all someday play in the National Football League.

It also used linebackers like Ryan Anderson, Rahsaan Evans, Ragland, and Tim Williams as pass-rushers, so the rotation was really more like 14 players.

Williams, who was largely overlooked because he wasn't considered an every-down player, might have been the best pass-rusher of the lot. He entered the playoffs with 9.5 sacks (11.5 tackles for a loss), which only trailed Allen's 10 (12.5).

"We chart not only sacks, but quarterback pressures, as well as batted balls," Saban said. "Those two things have been very good in terms of what the defensive line has been able to do, as well. They've been able to consistently make the quarterback uncomfortable and affect the way the guy has played, and I think that helps the secondary when the quarterback is not feeling like 'I can get in a rhythm, I got time, I can stand back here and wait for guys to come open.'"

In Alabama's official stats (the ones made public) Anderson led the team with 10 quarterback hurries, one more than Robinson although it's an unreliable gauge because of how they're credited. For example, Mississippi State acknowledged just four hurries for the Crimson Tide, three fewer than it had for the Bulldogs. The statisticians at A&T Stadium for the Wisconsin game had Alabama down for two, and Georgia's crew didn't credit a player from either team with one, which isn't uncommon.

As for batted passes, Alabama's linemen had 16, which was second only to UCLA in the NCAA. Junior Dalvin Tomlinson, who would be starting just about anywhere else, topped the Crimson Tide with six.

Another statistic that Alabama kept track of was quarterbacks hits, and Saban noted that in addition to the sacks, Mississippi State quarterback Dak Prescott got hit 12 more times and ran six quarterback scrambles.

"I'm proud of the way our defense played," Allen said. "It feels great when you execute the game plan, we did a hell of a job up front. But a lot of times it was cover sacks, so the DBs deserve a lot of credit. They were knocking down receivers and giving us a lot of time to get to the quarterback.

"So as good as we played, they played just as well."

But it all started up front, with Allen, Reed, and Robinson, and the waves of players behind them on the very deep depth chart.

"I don't know if they were doing anything special but just beating guys up there," Mississippi State coach Dan Mullen said. ∎

Alabama linebacker Tim Williams celebrates after sacking Michigan State quarterback Connor Cook in the third quarter of the Cotton Bowl.

ALABAMA SAYS GOODBYE TO A LEGEND

Crimson Tide Pays Tribute to Kenny Stabler

Although the winning ways continued, Bryant-Denny Stadium just wasn't the same during the 2015 season.

The warm smile, Southern gentlemanly disposition and silver hair were noticeably absent from the place that had essentially been his second home for 50-plus years. Granted, the trips had been fewer of late, but his presence and influence could always be felt. That part, at least, will never change.

When the University of Alabama hosted LSU it said goodbye with a special tribute to one of its fallen sons, heroes, and icons, Kenny Stabler, who died in July from complications associated with colon cancer. The former quarterback and National Football League star who bled Crimson and White as much as anyone was 69.

"He loved the University of Alabama; he truly did," said Stabler's oldest daughter Kendra Stabler Moyes, who along with the rest of the Stabler family was honored on the field during a pregame tribute. "He was proud to be from Alabama and of the University, and he always said so."

One would be hard-pressed to find a Crimson Tide fan anywhere who didn't have some sort of Stabler story, which only added to why his absence was so noticeable.

He was especially missed when the 50th anniversary of the 1965 national championship team was celebrated during Ole Miss weekend. Former teammates like Jerry Duncan could still hear his voice in their heads, like when he would enter a huddle and say something like: "Alright guys let's take this thing down here, knock it in and get us a touchdown and go out tonight and have a good time."

"He loved life and he loved to have a good time and he was a tremendous football player," Duncan surmised.

So many people, so many tales that will continue to be told and handed down.

"I've had the chance to be around some of the best to ever play college and pro football, and Kenny may have been one of the greatest competitors to ever play the game," Nick Saban said. "He was not only an outstanding football player, he was an all-around great guy and someone I really enjoyed spending time with. We lost a legend."

One retrospective comment that got Saban's attention in particular was from Stabler's former coach with the Oakland Raiders, John Madden. In addition to saying "The hotter the game, the cooler he got" about Stabler's demeanor, he still maintained that if he had one drive to win a game and could pick any quarterback, past or present, "Snake" was his man.

Saban called it the ultimate compliment for a quarterback.

"You think that Kenny is one of those guys that whatever you throw in front of him, it's not going to get him down. Then, when you hear Kenny Stabler died, it's like a kick in the gut," Madden told Raiders reporters in July.

"You think of the good times and the memories, all of the games and all of the practices and all of the meetings. No matter what you throw in front of him,

Alabama quarterback legend Kenny Stabler passed away at the age of 69 on July 8, 2015.

he enjoyed it. He always had a twinkle in his eye and a smile. He was one of the greatest competitors ever."

From 1973, when he took over the starting job, Stabler quarterbacked the Raiders to a 50-11-1 regular-season record over an amazing five years and helped lead a 32-14 victory over the Minnesota Vikings in Super Bowl XI.

Overall the left-hander played 10 seasons for the Raiders (1970-79), and also briefly with the Houston Oilers and New Orleans Saints, en route to 194 touchdown passes (222 interceptions) and 27,398 passing yards. His record as an NFL starter was 94-49-1, and Stabler ended up playing in more "name" games than anyone, including "The Ghost to the Post," "The Holy Roller," and "The Sea of Hands." Named All-Pro three times, he was the league's Offensive Player of the Year in 1974, and both the Player of the Year and passing champion in 1976.

But his legacy was also strong at Alabama, where he followed Joe Namath and Steve Sloan, and after taking over as the starting quarterback led the 11-0 season of 1966 that didn't result in a national championship. Pollsters instead rewarded Notre Dame for pulling off a tie at Michigan State, which will forever be a sore subject to Crimson Tide fans.

"That '66 team, he rarely got his uniform dirty at all because no one ever touched him," joked Duncan, which was ironic for the player known for the "Run in the Mud," a 47-yard touchdown that was the difference in a 7-3 victory against Auburn in the 1967 Iron Bowl.

Stabler compiled a collegiate starting record of 28-3-2, including a dominating 34-7 victory against Nebraska in the 1967 Sugar Bowl to be named the game's most valuable player. After his playing career concluded he again became a fixture in Tuscaloosa while working a color analyst for Alabama football games on the Crimson Tide Sports Network (1998-2007).

By then he was viewed as being more than a state treasure.

Stabler was born Christmas Day in 1945 in Foley, Alabama, where he was a highly regarded high school

player and after a long, winding touchdown run was first called "Snake" by coach Denzel Hollis. Over the years he raised a lot of money for local charities and spent most of his final years in the Gulf Shores area.

"There is no way to describe the pride an Alabama player feels in himself and the tradition of the school," Stabler once said about the love affair he had with the university and its fans, and his influence reached both near and far.

As a result, when the man who seemed to collect friends and memories like they were the most valuable commodities died, people reached out in droves any way they could, with the family receiving thousands of cards, emails and messages—including a heartfelt type-written note from actor Tom Hanks, who had grown up a Raiders fan, which ended with one of Stabler's favorite sayings: "Throw deep, baby." They were simply overwhelmed.

"We knew that he was loved, but we had no idea the magnitude," Moyes said. "They were from all over the world, from places like Japan and Germany, and the really cool thing was that 95 percent of the messages had the same theme, about how he made them feel. 'He made me feel so special.'"

That above all else may have been Stabler's greatest gift. Sure he played the rebel while leading the Raiders, often with a mischievous grin, and maybe he made as many headlines off the field as on. But when a game started he was all business, and when it was over he was all charm.

"Travelling the country with him was truly like traveling with a rock star," said Stabler's radio broadcast partner Eli Gold. "He'd walk through the airport, and it would take forever because folks would want his autograph, [would want to] take pictures and he'd never turn down a request for any of that. He was just one of those people that everybody knew.

"Kenny loved people, and people loved Kenny. If you didn't like Kenny Stabler you've got a problem. He was just a great, great guy. ... The fact that he's gone now is very, very sad." ■

Alabama quarterback Kenny Stabler accepts the Sugar Bowl Most Valuable Player trophy on Jan. 3, 1967, after leading Alabama to a 34-7 win over Nebraska. Stabler passed away on July 8, 2015.

ALABAMA 30, LSU 16
November 7, 2015 • Tuscaloosa, Alabama

TAKING IT TO 11

Crimson Tide Rock Bryant-Denny, Take Down No. 2 LSU

Anyone still want to complain about the University of Alabama's initial ranking by the College Football Playoff committee?

Days after there was a loud uproar about it having one-loss Alabama fourth, ahead of some still undefeated teams, the Crimson Tide more than proved to be worthy by dominating No. 2 LSU 30-16 at Bryant-Denny Stadium.

The game wasn't as close as the score indicated, either, and considering that it was Nick Saban's fifth straight win over Les Miles, including the 2012 BCS Championship Game that resulted in a 21-0 final score, it didn't take long for the consequences to be felt.

While Miles very nearly lost his job a couple of weeks later at the conclusion of the regular season, Alabama was secure knowing that all the pieces were in place to make another title run.

"I've always liked the grit of this team," Saban said. "I've always liked the way this team competes. We may not always execute right, and people can criticize the penalties and the negative plays that we have sometimes, but ability to overcome adversity has not been an issue with this group so far."

⟫⟫⟫ STATISTIC OF THE GAME

Take your pick. Alabama had huge statistical advantages across the board including first downs (28-12), rushing yards (250-54), total yards (434-182), and time of possession (39:27-20:33).

Against the team that was supposed to be able to physically match up against the Crimson Tide, and was said to have the best player in college football, Alabama simply dominated—like junior defensive lineman A'Shawn Robinson hurdling a set lineman to swat an extra-point attempt down kind of dominating.

It was better in all facets of the game and especially on the lines.

After pulling away in the third quarter it ended up with an advantage in total yards of 434-182, and LSU quarterback Brandon Harris completed just six passes.

Yet the most telling statistics all centered around the running backs, with Alabama junior Derrick Henry pounding out 210 rushing yards on 38 carries, and scoring three touchdowns.

LSU's Leonard Fournette, who appeared to have such a huge lead in the Heisman Trophy race that the debate was over who was in second, was limited to 31 rushing yards on 19 carries.

Coming in, Fournette was averaging 193.1 yards per game and his season low was 154, set two weeks previous against Western Kentucky. Before he popped an 18-yard run to set up his own touchdown in the fourth quarter his biggest gain was just four yards.

"The week leading up to it the guys in the locker room were, 'Man, I'm sick of hearing about this guy,'" senior linebacker Reggie Ragland said. "He's really good."

A strong indication that it was going to be the Crimson Tide's night occurred before kickoff. The moment Ole Miss lost to Arkansas, which meant that Alabama again controlled its future in the Southeastern

The stingy Alabama defense meets star LSU running back Leonard Fournette at the line. Alabama held Fournette to a season-low 31 yards rushing on the way to a 30-16 win.

Conference's western division race, the energy at Bryant-Denny Stadium went to its highest levels yet in 2015.

To use a Spinal Tap reference it went to 11.

For Saban, though, he knew it the first time LSU ran its bread-and-butter rushing play with Fournette. Not only did the defense not buckle, but it stuffed him.

Led by the defensive line Alabama had nine different players contribute to seven tackles for a loss, and LSU's longest possession of the game was a mere six plays. Overall, only two players finished with more than four tackles, safety Geno Matias-Smith with six and senior lineman Jarran Reed with five.

That's the statistical definition of swarming.

"I thought I was about to make one play and I saw Geno come out of nowhere and just thump him, and I was 'Ooohhh-we,'" Ragland said. "I thought we did a great job. Everyone wrapped him up and if you wrap him up you have a good chance."

Even Henry called his defense "Phenomenal," although his teammates were saying the same about him.

"I've been saying the whole time that he's an impressive, dude, and he deserves all the respect and the accolades that come with that," said senior quarterback Jake Coker, while sophomore left tackle Cam Robinson had no problem proclaiming whom he thought should be the new frontrunner for the Heisman after Henry had the third-most carries by a player in Alabama history.

As a bonus, Robinson could also look forward to his next trip home to Monroe, La., as well. After leading a strong group of recruits out of the bayou in 2014, which caused Fournette to half joke during the preseason what he wanted to do something different by staying home, the lineman had more than bragging rights.

"It's always fun for me," a smiling Cam Robinson said. "I don't have to worry about anybody riding me."

Alabama running back Kenyan Drake eludes LSU's Dwayne Thomas down the sideline. Drake finished with 68 yards rushing on 10 carries, along with three catches for 40 yards.

>>> **PLAY OF THE GAME**

>>> PLAY OF THE GAME

When senior linebacker Dillon Lee picked off LSU quarterback Brandon Harris on the first offensive play of the second half it was the beginning of the end for the Tigers. Four plays later Henry scored his second touchdown for a 20-10 lead and LSU never really recovered. Lee's pickoff was even more impressive considering he did so despite having an injured hand wrapped up.

Actually, none of the players on Alabama roster except for those who redshirted in 2011 knew what it's like to lose to LSU. The Game of the Century resulted in a 9-6 final score, and since then the Tigers have been outscored in the series 130-63.

Perhaps like that year a postseason rematch was possible, but this time LSU would have the difficult road and need some serious help from the field. A strong defense and a pounding running game could always take a lot of teams far, only it already knew that Alabama was better at both.

"We've never counted ourselves out and now we're back in control of our own destiny in the West," said senior linebacker Dillon Lee, the first player to pick off a Harris pass in 2015. "I think we're just getting better and better every week, but tonight especially. Compared to the rest of the season it was our most complete game."

Yet Alabama (8-1, 5-1 SEC) knew it could play better, and still had to dispatch Mississippi State, rival Auburn and Florida in the SEC Championship Game.

It did enjoy this one, though.

"It was crazy," kicker Adam Griffith said about the Alabama locker room. "It was probably the craziest since the national championship my freshman year."

"I've never seen our team so excited over a win like that, because they're a really good team," senior center Ryan Kelly said. "This was the last SEC home game for me at Bryant-Denny Stadium. You just couldn't ask for a better way to go out." ■

Crimson Tide senior linebacker Dillon Lee celebrates with his teammates after picking off LSU quarterback Brandon Harris. Lee added three tackles and a sack on the day.

ALABAMA 31, MISSISSIPPI STATE 6
November 14, 2015 • Starkville, Mississippi

STEPPING FORWARD

Crimson Tide, Henry Emerge as SEC, Heisman Frontrunners in Win Over Bulldogs

It was bounce out, a stiff-arm and then whole lot of open space, but when University of Alabama junior running back Derrick Henry finally stopped in the end zone he acted like it was no big deal.

Of course the rest of the Crimson Tide didn't feel the same way, or the visiting fans. The ones sitting by the south end zone at Davis Wade Stadium started chanting "Heis-man, Heis-man" as Henry casually walked off the field.

"It's a big win against a good team," Henry said after Alabama's decisive 31-6 victory against Mississippi State.

Consequently, it was time to stop calling Henry a contender or even the frontrunner for college football's most coveted award and crank that status up a little more.

After accumulating 204 rushing yards on 23 carries and scoring two touchdowns during a game Alabama's offense wasn't very good, it became his award to win or lose.

There just didn't appear to be anyone else who could beat him out, just like Dak Prescott couldn't overshadow him at home despite passing for 300 yards and having

a career-high 26 carries. That included nine sacks by Alabama as both defenses were zeroed in on stopping the other team's star player.

"Obviously their game plan was to stop us from running the ball," Alabama head coach Nick Saban said. "They were going to force the quarterback and receivers to make plays. We dropped about four and five balls on some of those plays.

"We just had to get to where we could run the ball, period."

Although Henry only had five carries for 13 rushing yards in the first quarter, when the Crimson Tide defense kept the Bulldogs off the scoreboard with a clutch goal-line stand, he and Alabama broke the game open over the subsequent 15 minutes.

It began with senior Cyrus Jones taking a low punt, making the first guy miss and, as Saban put it: "Was out the gate."

The 69-yard touchdown was followed by a freshman wide receiver Calvin Ridley turning a simple out pass into a 60-yard touchdown that exceeded Alabama's total yards in the game before that play. Henry got into the mix by breaking a 74-yard touchdown that seemed to suck all of the energy out of the stadium.

It was also his 15th straight game scoring a rushing touchdown, topping Tim Tebow's impressive string at Florida in 2006-07.

⟩⟩⟩ PLAY OF THE GAME

The 69-yard punt return for a touchdown by Cyrus Jones was the first of his career and with the subsequent extra point provided the only points Alabama would need. He was also credited with four tackles and broke up two passes.

Derrick Henry fights off Mississippi State defensive back Kivon Coman and defensive lineman Nick James during Alabama's 31-6 win. Henry had another huge day with 204 yards on the ground and two touchdowns.

Meanwhile, Alabama's defense had another terrific game despite finishing at a disadvantage in total yards (393-379), time of possession (33:30-26:30), and first downs (20-13).

Yet the Bulldogs never got into the end zone.

"We thought the one thing that might be in our favor in this game was our defensive line against their offensive line," Saban said. "We did most of it with four guys rushing."

In other words, Alabama didn't blitz much, and really couldn't with Prescott's ability to run. The quarterback took a pounding and after numerous near-misses finally had a pass picked off late in the game, with prize wide receiver De'Runnya Wilson staying down after tackling freshman cornerback Marlon Humphrey on the return.

Before Wilson was carted, off Henry was one of the Alabama players checking on him.

"I was just praying for him," he said.

The interception, just Prescott's second of the season, came right after Henry's 65-yard touchdown to top the 200-yard mark, making him the first Alabama running back to do so in back-to-back games.

Both opponents were ranked too, LSU second and Mississippi State at No. 17. This was the sixth ranked opponent Alabama had faced and against them Henry averaged 178.7 rushing yards (1,072 total). The running back topped 125 against all of them and notched 200 against three. In those games he'd also tallied 154 carries, a 6.9-yard average per carry and scored 12 touchdowns.

Those are Heisman-type numbers.

Overall, Henry had rushed for 1,458 yards and 19 touchdowns. If he continued at that pace he'd finish the regular season with 1,750 rushing yards and 23 touchdowns, which would be school records (Trent Richardson 1,679 and 21, respectively, in 2011).

"That's the kind of back that he is," Saban said about the last touchdown. "As long as he is he does a good job of picking his way through holes, but once he gets rolling he's fast. He's faster than people think and faster than he looks.

"What you can always tell is he outruns the angles, and that's when you know that someone's pretty fast."

Alabama (9-1, 6-1 SEC) wouldn't pad his numbers either. Even with reserve running back Kenyan Drake suffering a fractured arm that would keep him out a couple of weeks, freshmen Damien Harris and Bo Scarbrough figured to get a lot of reps in the next game against Charleston Southern.

Freshman defensive back Minkah Fitzpatrick sustained a sprained knee that could keep him out a week, senior quarterback Jake Coker left the stadium with ice on his right shoulder and junior defensive lineman A'Shawn Robinson's left foot was in a boot.

Even Saban had a cut on his cheek when junior defensive lineman Jonathan Allen collided with the coach during a quick substitution.

"The athlete that I am I was able to keep my feet," Saban said. "The players were really concerned but they know they don't make them like they used to."

They also don't make them like Henry, who was contained by Mississippi State (7-3, 3-3 SEC) for a good part of the game, but not all.

"We knew eventually he was going to hit," senior center Ryan Kelly said. ∎

⟫⟫⟫ PLAYER OF THE GAME

Junior running back Derrick Henry topped 200 rushing yards for the second straight week with 204 on 22 carries and two touchdowns, of 74 and 65 yards. He averaged 9.3 yards per carry.

Quarterback Jake Coker targets receiver Calvin Ridley for a short pass. The catch, which went for 76 yards and a touchdown, was one of five for Ridley.

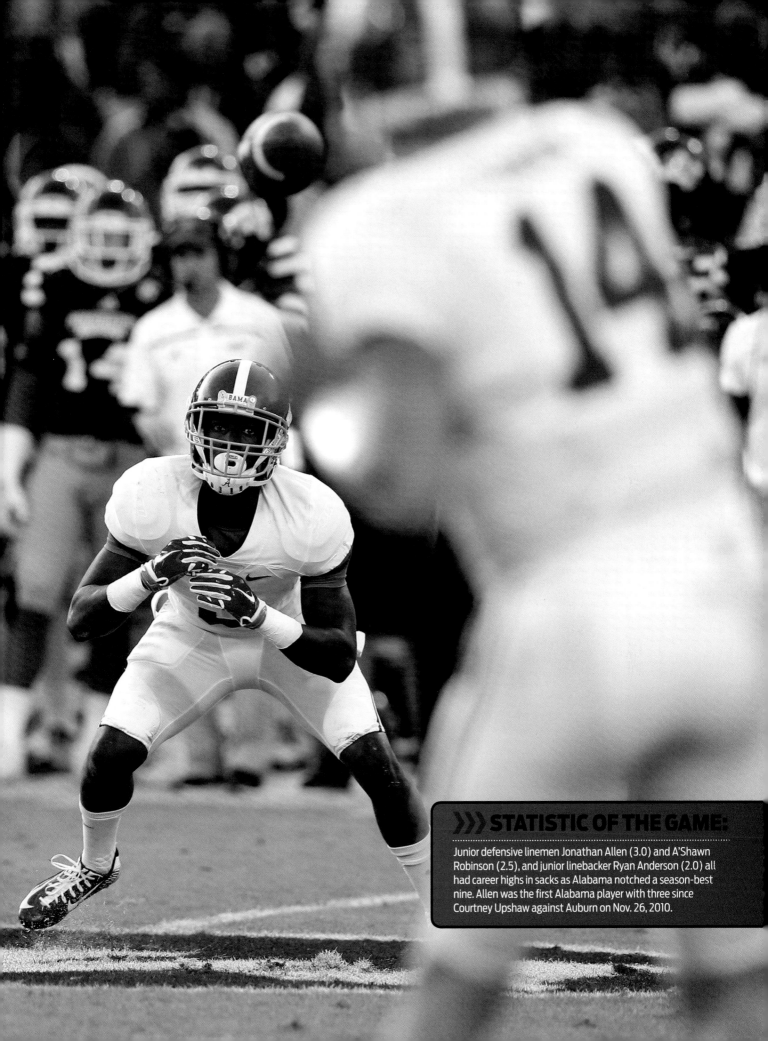

ALABAMA'S UNSUNG HEROES

Crimson Tide's Less Heralded Players Essential to Team's Success

They call him Highway 46.

It was in reference to what he often said on the field, "Highway 70 all the way," about the University of Alabama's offensive line and especially Ryan Kelly. The Crimson Tide did a lot of running behind the Rimington Award-winning senior center who wore No. 70, while No. 46 contributed quite a bit as well.

"Nyse is Highway 46 because if you get behind him he's going to block for you," junior tight end O.J. Howard said. "He's going to lead the way, so I think it fits him perfect."

If you've never heard of Michael Nysewander, you're not alone. He wasn't recruited by the Crimson Tide, walking on after playing at Hoover High School just outside of Birmingham. He then spent three years on Alabama's scout team before earning a spot on special teams in 2014.

That led to opportunities on offense, as a traditional tight end, H-back and fullback—whatever necessary. Alabama didn't really have a lead blocker for running back Derrick Henry in short-yardage situations so when Nick Saban offered a chance to play a fifth year on scholarship Nysewander quickly accepted.

"If I had five more years of eligibility I think I'd play five more years if I could," Nysewander said. "It was really a no-brainer.

"I know when I first came here I tried to set individual goals for myself. I think the first one was I just want Coach Saban to learn my name. Second was to win some scout-team player awards, stuff like that. I've tried to build a little bit as I go, but I think it's been a great career."

Overall, Alabama's unsung hero had played in 21 games heading into the 2015 playoffs, with seven tackles and three receptions, but two were for touchdowns.

The first came in 2014 against Western Carolina after Alabama had pulled all of its starters. The second was with six minutes and six seconds remaining on the clock in the third quarter of the 34-0 victory over Louisiana-Monroe.

Celebrating teammates mobbed Nysewander and Saban later admitted on his radio show that it almost made him cry on the sideline.

"He's just one of those throwback players to me," Saban said. "You've got to love him. I get a smile on my face every time I talk about him. He's just a tough grinder."

Although it was his only reception of the 2015 regular season, time and time again No. 46 was on the field when the Crimson Tide made a big play. One of the more noticeable was on Henry's third touchdown run against LSU when Nysewander provided the lead block.

"He flattened the guy. He knocked the guy down and pancaked him," Howard said.

"He started high-stepping. The celebration was pretty funny, too."

The friendly grief from teammates was, as Nysewander explained, because "standing next to Derrick, who's 6-3, and my short little legs going about a million miles per hour."

Senior tight end Michael Nysewander lines up against Mississippi State on Nov. 14. Nysewander plays many roles on the Crimson Tide but is best known for his lead blocking for running back Derrick Henry.

Although the 2015-16 Crimson Tide will be forever remembered for its impressive title run and Henry's Heisman Trophy, the seniors had already accomplished quite a lot including at least one national championship (two for those who redshirted in 2011), and two Southeastern Conference titles before topping Florida for a third.

The worst postseason game that any of them played in was the Sugar Bowl. The group also extended Alabama's streak of 10-plus wins in a season to a record eighth straight year.

The class included prominent names like Kelly, Reggie Ragland, and Jarran Reed, who were expected to be high NFL draft selections in the spring. Linebacker Denzel Devall made his first start as a sophomore in 2013, while players like Kenyan Drake, Darren Lake, and Dillon Lee all made their mark.

But there was also of host of other players who worked just as hard without anywhere near the same kind of recognition.

Among them, Parker Barrineau was a regular part of the upper tier in the receiving corps during practices for three years, during which he spent a lot of time helping Alabama's younger players get up to speed and improve.

Unfortunately, surgery to repair a bad cut on his foot slowed the recruited walk-on during training camp of his final season, but he was still a regular on special teams and most of his playing time on offense had been as a blocker.

In a way Nysewander's touchdown was for him too, and all of the players who didn't get a lot of attention including the reserves, scout-team regulars, walk-ons and even role players. That's why the whole team got so excited.

"He's everything that anybody things that a football player or a competitor should be, in terms of work ethic, doing the right things, always giving 100 percent, always trying to pay attention to do things right, puts the team first all of the time," Saban said. "I think he's very well liked by his teammate, he cares more about the team more than he cares about himself. I don't know if he ever asked a question, 'What about me? How much am I going to play.' He's always, 'What can I do for the team?'

"I can't think of one thing that I would say that if you were looking for the perfect attitude player on your team that he wouldn't fit that. The guy is really tough and he plays as close to his full potential as anybody on our team because of the character and attitude he competes with."

That's what made Nysewander so special and why he was voted by teammates the winner of the Crimson Tide's Most Inspirational Player award. He's also a big reason why Saban called this senior class a special one, because a college football team can't win without players like them.

Not everyone could be Coker or wide receiver Richard Mullaney, graduate transfers filling specific needs. Cyrus Jones and Bradley Sylve switched from wide receiver to cornerback when the Crimson Tide had depth issues in the secondary, and it took a move to free safety for Geno Matias-Smith to land regular starting spot during his final year. From Alex Harrelson, who filled in two games for long-snapper Cole Mazza, to defensive back Jabriel Washington, a lot of seniors played a part in the team's success.

It took a lot more than big bodies like Dominick Jackson and D.J. Pettway for the Crimson Tide to be like a truck barreling through opponents. It took a convoy of players like Nysewander.

"I really like the fight and the grit that this team has," he said.

"Highway 46," the Heisman Trophy winner said with a smile. "I'm rocking with him the whole way." ∎

Michael Nysewander rolls out to block for Derrick Henry against LSU. Nysewander is a favorite among teammates and was voted the winner of the Crimson Tide's Most Inspirational Player award.

ALABAMA 56, CHARLESTON SOUTHERN 6
November 21, 2015 • Tuscaloosa, Alabama

'THE TIN-HORN GAME'

No Letdown as Crimson Tide Thoroughly Dominates FCS Opponent

It will forever be known as the tin-horn game because that's the way the University of Alabama went through Charleston Southern.

Four days after head coach Nick Saban made it clear that he wasn't going to accept any sort of a letdown against a Football Championship Series opponent the Crimson Tide lived up to his expectations and absolutely destroyed the Buccaneers 56-6 at Bryant-Denny Stadium.

"We heard it all right before you heard it," senior linebacker Reggie Ragland said about the Saban rant during a press conference. "We couldn't take anything for granted, we had to play hard. That's all they talked about all week."

Considering what No. 2 Alabama (10-1) was still playing for, including a shot at the playoffs if it could beat both Auburn and Florida in the SEC Championship Game, Saban wasn't going to take any chances—especially the way the Crimson Tide was playing down the stretch.

So on Wednesday, when asked about Charleston Southern quarterback Austin Brown he brought up

how the 2011 Crimson Tide defense that finished first in all four major statistical categories (total, scoring, rushing and pass-efficiency defense) struggled against Georgia Southern's option attack: "They ran through our (expletive) like (expletive) through a tin horn, man, and we could not stop them."

However, the game ended up giving him another motivational tool down the road as senior cornerback Cyrus Jones demonstrated how someone should play in his last home game.

Not only did he return two punts for touchdowns, making him the first Crimson Tide player to do so since Alabama started keeping records on returns in 1944, but he also deflected an option pitch to himself for a fumble recovery. Jones subsequently returned it 18 yards to set up Alabama's seventh touchdown of the first half.

"I was saying all game I was going to jump his option," Jones said.

The punt returns were just as impressive, of 43 and 72 yards, the first after the ball appeared to deflect off teammate Maurice Smith and into open field. Jones promptly ran over, grabbed the ball and kept going.

"Coming in we knew that that punter was going to do a rugby-style punt, a lot of line drives and you had to play them off the bounce," Jones said. "I actually thought it was going to take a big hop only it hit Mo in the foot. I just tried to pick it up and make a play."

It was that kind of day for the overmatched visitors, who at the break had 31 total yards of offense

>>> PLAY OF THE GAME

Cyrus Jones became the first player since Alabama started compiling special-teams records in 1944 to score twice in a game on punt returns. With his 43-yard return he notched the first punt returns for a touchdown in consecutive weeks by the same player, and later added a 72-yard return for a touchdown.

The dominant Alabama defense piles on Charleston Southern quarterback Kyle Copeland in the Tide's 56-6 non-conference romp.

>>> PLAYER OF THE GAME

Senior cornerback Cyrus Jones had a monster sendoff game with two punt returns for touchdowns, three tackles, all for a loss, a forced fumble and a fumble recovery when he interrupted an option pitch in the backfield.

compared to Alabama's 49 points.

"Well, the outcome was probably what we expected," Charleston Southern coach Jamey Chadwell said.

"They're obviously as good as anybody we've seen. I don't know if you could combine all of the teams we played and [equal] all of their best players. I do think we had more yards rushing than Leonard Fournette did, though, so you can check that. But we couldn't run up inside."

LSU's Fournette rushed for 31 yards on 19 carries against the Alabama defense on Nov. 7, for an average of 1.6 yards. CSU had 31 yards on 21 carries at halftime, and zero passing, with the Crimson Tide already inserting reserves. The Bucs (9-2) finished with 85 rushing yards on 36 carries and barely avoided the shutout.

On the flip side, Alabama running back Derrick Henry could have all but called his rushing numbers for the day. He had just nine carries for 68 rushing yards, a 28-yard reception and two touchdowns.

The first extended his streak of games with a rushing touchdown to 16, and the second tied Trent Richardson's record for rushing touchdowns in a single season with 21.

Henry also went over the 1,500-yard mark for the season and despite his limited use might have only tightened his grip on the Heisman Trophy. Ohio State running back Ezekiel Elliott, arguably Henry's most

serious challenger, only had 33 rushing yards on 12 carries during the 17-14 loss to Michigan State.

Like starting quarterback Jake Coker, who completed 11 of 13 passes for 155 yards and two touchdowns, Henry was pulled in the second quarter.

"We did what we needed to do and were real efficient," Coker said.

Otherwise, the home finale was a day for the seniors and the players who don't get on the field too often, with sophomore Cooper Bateman and junior Alec Morris getting turns at quarterback, senior cornerback Bradley Sylve leading the Crimson Tide in solo tackles with four, and senior defensive back Jabriel Washington making an interception.

"It was great," Washington said. "I saw the end zone too. I was one person away."

Overall, the senior class had compiled a 46-5 record over four years, but everyone knows that Alabama teams are remembered for their ring collections. This one was showing strong signs that it wanted some.

"I'm glad I went out the way I did," Jones said. ■

Coach Nick Saban reacts to a play in Alabama's Nov. 21 victory over Charleston Southern. The win brought Alabama's record to 10-1 on the season

IRON BOWL

ALABAMA 29, AUBURN 13
November 28, 2015 • Auburn, Alabama

RE-WRITING THE RECORD BOOK

Henry Rushes for 271 Yards, Tide Seals Spot in SEC Championship Game

Every time Derrick Henry came off the field in the fourth quarter Nick Saban was there to check on him. As the carries mounted and started approaching previously unseen levels at Alabama the conversation kept repeating itself.

"Are you good? Are you tired?" the head coach kept asking.

"I'm good," was always the response.

Actually, he was great as No. 2 Alabama wrapped up the Southeastern Conference's West Division title to secure its spot in the SEC Championship Game against Florida.

With a record-setting performance Henry finished with 46 carries for 271 rushing yards and a late touchdown as Alabama won it annual showdown with Auburn 29-13 at Jordan-Hare Stadium.

The junior running back earned every bit of it as well. The carries were a single-game record at Alabama. The yards were an Iron Bowl rushing record and it was the 17th straight game in which he'd reached the end zone.

Moreover, with potentially three games to go Henry became the Crimson Tide's all-time leader for rushing yards in a season with 1,797, topping Trent Richardson's 1,679 in 2011.

"It means a lot to me, my teammates, the offensive line, everyone on the offense that worked hard to get here, to accomplish something so big," Henry said. "We just had to stay locked in and focused."

While Henry averaged 5.9 yards per attempt his longest gain was just 30 yards, which was a testament to how tough those carries were.

Alabama (11-1, 7-1 SEC) executed 21 plays in the fourth quarter and all but two were handoffs to Henry. Auburn knew what was coming with every snap and he still churned out 114 rushing yards over the final 15 minutes.

"I didn't realize it because we didn't have any long runs, but that shows how durable he is, and how strong he is to be able to pound it non-stop," senior quarterback Jake Coker said. "He's like a machine."

Henry almost certainly ended the Heisman Trophy chase as well after becoming one of only three backs

>>> PLAY OF THE GAME

Anyone who knew Adam Griffith's back story couldn't help but be happy for the one-time Polish orphan when he drilled the 50-yard field goal at the site of the Kick Six game in 2013. His five field goals set an Alabama record in the Iron Bowl and were the second most in a single game by a Crimson Tide kicker. He had made 19 of his last 22 field-goal attempts, all 48 extra-point attempts in 2015 and a career-best 42 touchbacks on kickoffs.

Alabama kicker Adam Griffith winds up for the kick in the Crimson Tide's 29-13 win over Auburn in the Iron Bowl. Griffith was perfect on the day, going five-for-five on field goals and two-for-two on extra points.

PLAYER OF THE GAME

Derrick Henry's 271 rushing yards made him the first Alabama running back to notch 250 or more since Shaun Alexander in 1996 (291 at LSU). It was the third-most yards in a single game, behind only Alexander and Bobby Humphrey's 284 at Mississippi State in 1986.

in Southeastern Conference history with four games of 200 yards or more in a season, joining Herschel Walker (Georgia) and Bo Jackson (Auburn).

LSU's Leonard Fournette had three earlier in the season against Auburn (19 carries for 228 yards), Syracuse, and Eastern Michigan.

"We'd really like for somebody else to run the ball, but it got tough to take him out and he seemed to get stronger as the game goes on," Saban said.

"He's the go-to-guy and he didn't want to come out. My hat's off to him as a competitor. He really inspires everyone on our team the way he competes and the way he plays, the toughness that he runs with. What a spirit."

Henry's performance was in spite of poor field conditions as numerous players on both sides slipped when trying to make cuts. Consequently, the first half essentially turned into a Punt, Pass & Kick competition only without the first two parts.

Instead, with Henry gaining 106 rushing yards on 16 carries in the first half and Coker connecting with freshman Calvin Ridley for a 46-yard deep pass, junior kicker Adam Griffith appeared to vanquish whatever demons might still be lingering from the Kick Six game in 2013 with four of his five field goals.

They were, in order, from 26, 40, 26, and 50 yards when Auburn put someone in the end zone for a possible return—and don't think Alabama didn't notice.

"I didn't think I had a monkey on my back," Griffith said. Yet he still had a lot of teammates congratulate him after making that particular one with room to spare, and later hit a fifth field goal in the second half, from 47 yards.

Meanwhile, his counterpart Daniel Carlson connected from 24 and 44 yards, but missed from 48. Auburn's passing game was essentially held to two first-half completions to running backs, as Melvin Ray's 8-yard catch on third-and-10 was the lone reception by a wide receiver.

Consequently, Alabama came very close to putting the game out of reach early in the third

Derrick Henry breaks free for an Alabama touchdown, helping the Crimson Tide beat Auburn and clinch the SEC West. Henry was a workhorse on the day, finishing with 46 carries for 271 yards and one touchdown.

>>> **STATISTIC OF THE GAME**

Auburn converted only 3 of 15 third-down opportunities, including 0-for-4 for minus-18 yards in the fourth quarter due to two sacks, an incomplete pass and a lost fumble.

quarter when it finally reached the end zone.

Shortly after a Coker scramble sophomore wide receiver ArDarius Stewart—who had dropped a pass in the end zone and appeared to run the wrong route on a third down—had man coverage wide and the quarterback saw it. After avoiding two pass-rushers he threw a dart to the wide receiver for a 34-yard touchdown.

"Amazing," Coker said about playing in the Iron Bowl. "Indescribable."

Facing third-and-12 at its own 23, Auburn may have been a play away from essentially waving the white flag when wide receiver Jason Smith did his own version of the 2013 miracle catch against Georgia, tipping the ball twice to himself in open space en route to a 77-yard touchdown.

With its marching band playing Bon Jovi's "Livin' on a Prayer" Auburn had new life, only to get trampled by Henry down the stretch. With senior Kenyan Drake still on the mend with an arm fracture the only other Crimson Tide running back to have a carry was freshman Damien Harris with one.

"What Derrick has done for this team, because this team has needed him to do what he does, he's made as significant impact on his team as any player we've ever had," said Saban, who coached the 2009 Heisman Trophy winner, Mark Ingram Jr.

The most carries in a game that Ingram had that season was 28, and he only had one 200-yard rushing performance (South Carolina, 246).

"The guy never gets tired," senior center Ryan Kelly said about Henry. "We ran the ball a lot and it was good to see him get the touchdown."

Maybe the question should have been could anyone stop him? The same couldn't have been said of anyone else in college football in 2015.

"I don't know," Henry said. "I'm just trying to make plays." ∎

Derrick Henry greets fans after the huge 'Bama win. Henry's big day rushing allowed him to break Trent Richardson's single-season rushing mark for the school, which stood at 1,679 yards.

SEC CHAMPIONSHIP GAME
ALABAMA 29, FLORIDA 15
December 5, 2015 • Atlanta, Georgia

PLAYOFF PAYOFF

Henry, Defense Lead Tide to Second Consecutive SEC Championship

Derrick Henry put a cap on arguably the best season a running back has ever had in the Southeastern Conference, but that's not what should scare the other teams that might make this season's playoffs.

It's that the University of Alabama football team was so much more than Henry as it pounded out a 29-15 victory in the SEC Championship Game.

The No. 2 Crimson Tide had contributions from every part of the team in the Georgia Dome, on offense, defense, and special teams. Together they showed that they're still hungry, in addition to being the league's first repeat champions since Tennessee in 1997-98.

"After the Ole Miss game these players all said they wanted to be a different team," head coach Nick Saban said. "They wanted to do something special. Probably more than any other time I've coached I wanted to see those guys succeed today and win the second back-to-back SEC Championship and have an opportunity to get into the playoff."

Granted, Henry was terrific as usual.

With 189 yards on 44 carries—yes, giving him 90 attempts for the past two games alone—Henry's 1,986 rushing yards for the season were the most in SEC history.

The guy who used to have the record? Herschel Walker (1,891 yards on 385 carries in 1981).

Henry also became the first player to have a second 100-yard rushing performance in the SEC Championship Game, and his 2-yard rushing touchdown was his 23rd of the season to tie another league record.

The guys to hold that one with him are Tre Mason and Tim Tebow.

"I think that's the best defense that we faced," Henry said after giving credit to his coaches and teammates and before heading to Atlanta and New York to pick up a lot of hardware. "They're very physical, disruptive, very fast on the defensive line. Athletic linebackers who are very physical and try to knock you out, and good secondary."

But Henry wasn't a one-man wrecking crew as No. 18 Florida was determined to make Alabama (12-1) find other ways to win the game. The thing is, it did.

In the first half alone Alabama had a blocked punt for a safety by redshirt freshman linebacker Keith Holcombe, and senior defensive lineman D.J. Pettway subsequently blocked a field goal.

"It was slo-mo, yet at the same time it happened so quickly. I didn't even have time to think about it," Holcombe said.

⟫⟫ PLAY OF THE GAME

Even though he was double-covered on the play, freshman wide receiver Calvin Ridley leaped between them to make a clutch 55-yard catch at the Florida 3 just before halftime. Alabama was down 7-5 at the time and it set up Henry's 2-yard touchdown. Ridley finished with eight catches for 102 yards.

Nick Saban, Derrick Henry (left), and the Crimson Tide celebrate their victory over Florida in the SEC Championship Game. Henry was named the game's MVP with 189 yards rushing and one touchdown.

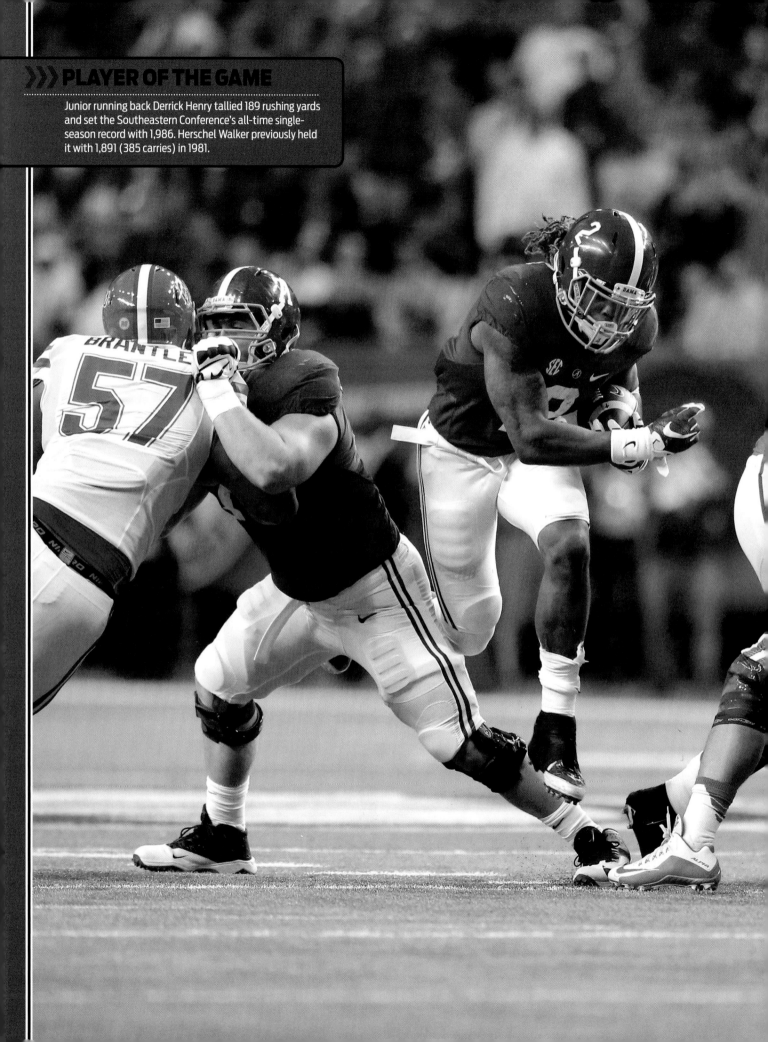

>>> **PLAYER OF THE GAME**

Junior running back Derrick Henry tallied 189 rushing yards
and set the Southeastern Conference's all-time single-
season record with 1,986. Herschel Walker previously held
it with 1,891 (385 carries) in 1981.

Alabama did give up a 75-yard punt return for a touchdown by Antonio Calloway, giving the Gators a short-lived 7-2 lead, but that was really just one of three highlights for Florida. The other two were a 46-yard bomb to Callaway (his only reception of the game), and a late 46-yard touchdown pass to C.J. Worton that caused the Crimson Tide coaches to reinsert the starters to kill the clock.

Those two completions accounted for 51 percent of Florida's offense (180 total yards).

"My hat's off to an outstanding Alabama Crimson Tide team that took our offense out of it," said Saban's former offensive coordinator Jim McElwain, Florida's first-year head coach. "I thought our defense battled their tails off."

He later added: "Shoot guys, they won the line of scrimmage. That's what big, strong, highly recruited guys do. That's why we're getting on the road as soon as we leave right now."

The Gators (10-3) finished with just 15 rushing yards and didn't convert a single third-down opportunity. Quarterback Treon Harris completed just 9 of 24 passes and was sacked five times.

From the end of the first quarter through Florida's first possession of the final period (13:16 left in the game), Alabama's defense gave up just three yards of total offense. During that time span the Crimson Tide scored 27 unanswered points.

Freshman wide receiver Calvin Ridley had the reception of the night, when despite having two defenders on him, including standout cornerback Vernon Hargreaves III, he came down with the clutch 55-yard catch at the Florida 3 just before halftime. Two plays later Henry extended his streak of having at least one rushing touchdown to 18 games.

Ridley finished with eight catches for 102 yards while sophomore wide receiver ArDarius Stewart had a terrific leaping

Derrick Henry hits the hole in the Tide's 29-15 win over the Gators. Henry continued his assault on the record books as he tied the SEC record for touchdowns at 23 and broke Herschel Walker's 34-year-old single-season conference rushing mark.

grab for a 32-yard touchdown and senior wideout Richard Mullaney helped complete Alabama's scoring with a 9-yard catch. Senior quarterback Jake Coker was 18-for-26 for 204 yards and ran for 23 more despite being sacked twice.

The Crimson Tide's other offensive weapon was also an important one, senior running back Kenyan Drake, who got the ball on Alabama's very first snap. After suffering a fractured arm at Mississippi State on Nov. 14 he still couldn't hold a ball or make blocks until a few days before the game, and still wore a protective pad over a surgical scar that went a good part of his forearm.

"I set my goal to be back at the SEC Championship," Drake said. "It wasn't on them, it was really on me."

Add that all together and it was too much for Florida to counter and served notice that Alabama would be much tougher to knock out of the playoffs than last year, especially considering the way the Crimson Tide had handled numerous potential distractions.

From the Heisman talk to defensive coordinator Kirby Smart being hired at Georgia to be Mark Richt's replacement, none of it seemed to phase the Crimson Tide.

"He said he's staying with us, he'll be with us for the next couple of games," senior cornerback Cyrus Jones about Smart.

There's also this to consider: Alabama could rest up before playing in either the Cotton Bowl or Orange Bowl at the end of the month, including Henry.

"I can't tell you how proud I am of this guy," Saban said. "He's had a phenomenal season and he deserves every accolade that anyone could ever throw his way." ∎

Alabama wide receiver ArDarius Stewart leaps over Florida linebacker Antonio Morrison. Stewart finished with four receptions for 64 yards and a touchdown.

RUNNING BACK

DERRICK HENRY

Heisman Trophy Fulfills Lifelong Dream for Unstoppable Back

Although he was quiet about it until the very end, winning a Heisman Trophy had always been on Derrick Henry's mind.

When the University of Alabama running back starting playing football at age five he used to pretend that someday his name would be synonymous with the legendary award. That continued in the video game world as Henry would always be among the first to purchase EA Sports' NCAA Football every year, and then try and win the Heisman with either a version of himself that he created or a player on a good team.

"It'd mean everything, man. It'd be a dream come true. It makes my heart beat just thinking about it," Henry said about the possibility of winning after being named one of three finalists for college football biggest award along with Stanford's Christian McCaffrey and Clemson's Deshaun Watson.

"It's been a lifelong goal, a dream of mine since I was a little kid, and just to be in that Heisman brotherhood would be unbelievable."

Actually, what was unbelievable was the way that Henry played down the stretch, continuing to run down and over opponents who were dug in and still unable to stop him. A perfect example was against rival Auburn, when Alabama's final 14 play-calls were the exact same, handoff to No. 2.

"Derrick wasn't tired," said senior linebacker Reggie Ragland, who enjoyed watching every moment of it. "Derrick kept running harder as he going. That's the type of guy he is, his mindset goes up when the competition goes up. When it's crunch time, it's eating time."

"It's like playing with the biggest guy on the playground, like 'What are you going to do to stop this guy?' It's just about impossible. The guy is crazy," senior quarterback Jake Coker said. "It's awesome to have a guy like that in the backfield and know he's on your side."

Derrick Henry leaps during a run in a 27-14 win over Arkansas. Henry rushed for 95 yards and a touchdown in the game on his way to winning the 2015 Heisman Trophy, just the third running back in the past 16 years to do so.

THE HEISMAN MEMORIAL TROPHY
PRESENTED BY
THE HEISMAN TROPHY TRUST
TO
DERRICK HENRY
THE UNIVERSITY OF ALABAMA
AS THE OUTSTANDING COLLEGE FOOTBALL PLAYER
IN THE UNITED STATES FOR
2015

Henry finished that record-setting night with 46 carries for 271 rushing yards and a touchdown as Alabama won its annual showdown 29-13 at Jordan-Hare Stadium.

The carries were single-game record for the Crimson Tide, while the yards were an Iron Bowl rushing record. He capped it off with his 22nd rushing touchdown of the season, another Alabama record, making it the 17th straight game in which Henry had reached the end zone.

"It was like watching Jack Morris pitch into extra innings," CBS announcer Gary Danielson while referring to Game 7 of the 1991 World Series, when the ace threw 10 scoreless inning as the Minnesota Twins beat the Atlanta Braves 1-0.

Moreover, even before the SEC Championship Game he became the Crimson Tide's all-time leader for rushing yards in a single season with 1,797, topping Trent Richardson's 1,679 in 2011, and all but became a lock to win the Heisman Trophy.

Mark Ingram Jr. won the program's first in 2009, but Henry became one of only three running backs in Southeastern Conference history with four games of 200 rushing yards or more in a season, joining Georgia's Herschel Walker and Auburn's Bo Jackson.

Yet it was really nothing new for his teammates. Henry started terrifying them before even taking the field for the first time.

It was January 2013, and the super-prospect was an early enrollee. The hype surrounding Henry was nothing short of suffocating and reminiscent of what has been experienced by former wide receiver Julio Jones, another five-star prospect whom fans couldn't wait to see playing on Saturdays.

Despite being a running back Henry was listed as 6-foot-3, 242 pounds, roughly Eddie George's size when he won the Heisman at Ohio State in 1995. He had also just broken Ken Hall's 51-year-old national high school rushing record with 12,124 career yards after totaling 4,261 as a senior in Yulee, Fla., and named the national player of the year by the Maxwell Football Club, Parade Magazine, the Columbus (Ohio) Touchdown Club and MaxPreps.

Yet it was Henry's work ethic that really got everyone's attention at the Capstone.

"He's just a freak," tight end O.J. Howard said at the time. "He's my roommate and he scares me sometimes just walking around.

"He's a guy who works really hard. He gets up at night and does push-ups."

Pretty soon they'd see that same effort both in and out of the weight room, like when he'd push trucks around a track and flip monster-truck tires around over the summer. Henry never seemed to let up, not even during a spring-break trip, when he led teammates through some drills on the beach at Panama City.

"I just didn't want to miss a beat. You know what I'm saying?" Henry said. "We were having fun, but I was like 'Hey we gotta get some work in.' So we started doing push-ups running in the sand, just doing anything to get us in a sweat to make us feel good and that's what we did.

"I just love working hard. I feel like hard work, if you want things to happen you gotta work hard for them."

That drive and determination was something that didn't waver as Henry developed from being the guy just beginning to figure out what playing at this level entailed to the featured running back on a perennial national contender.

HEISMAN TROPHY VOTING

Player	School	First	Second	Third	Total
Derrick Henry	Alabama	378	277	144	1,832
Christian McCaffrey	Stanford	290	246	177	1,539
Deshaun Watson	Clemson	148	240	241	1,165
Baker Mayfield	Oklahoma	34	55	122	334
Keenan Reynolds	Navy	20	17	86	180
Leonard Fournette	LSU	10	25	30	110
Dalvin Cook	Florida St.	7	18	22	79
Ezekiel Elliott	Ohio State	5	7	28	57
Connor Cook	Michigan St.	2	3	1	13
Trevone Boykin	TCU	1	3	4	13

Derrick Henry poses with the Heisman Trophy. Henry joined fellow Alabama running back Mark Ingram, Jr. as the only Heisman winners in school history.

It didn't happen overnight, though, as Henry concedes that he wasn't quite ready for all that as a freshman, especially the every-down responsibilities and doing all of the little things that hadn't previously been required of him. He improved in those areas, like stonewalling blitzers and blocking assignments, as much as any other.

"He has a real burning desire to be a really, really good player and works really hard at it," said Nick Saban, who had a tough time pulling Henry after he started punishing defenses in second half—when no one wanted anything to do with the fast-moving guy wearing size 14 shoes who's bigger than most linebackers.

"He's got the endurance," senior center Ryan Kelly said. "I mean, the guy can run for days. Defensive guys, when we start going fast in the third and fourth quarter, them getting off the ground, running back there, trying to get lined up, then you've got Derrick Henry running at you and you have to tackle him, do it all over again, that kind of wears down defenders.

"I can't say for them, but a guy like his stature, his size, his speed, I wouldn't want to do that every time. It would suck."

Ask LSU, when Henry had 210 rushing yards and then-Heisman frontrunner Leonard Fournette only tallied 31. Or Texas A&M (236). Or Mississippi State (204). Or Auburn …

Combine those performances along with breaking Walker's SEC rushing record, leading the league in rushing in conference games with a 179.2 yards average, tallying 180.1 per game against ranked teams and 144.4 versus eight rushing defenses ranked in the top 50 nationally, and averaging 105.3 yards per game after contact (69 percent of rushing yards), and no one was surprised when Henry was named the winner.

He then gave a 10-minute acceptance speech from the heart, thanking everyone from Saban to even one of his former teammates, Altee Tenpenny.

"He's been a brother to me who died this year," Henry said at the end of his speech. "I just want to tell him I love him and I miss him and God bless. Roll Tide." ∎

Derrick Henry celebrates and points at the crowd after scoring a touchdown in Alabama's 37-10 rout of Middle Tennessee on Sept. 12.

COTTON BOWL
ALABAMA 38, MICHIGAN STATE 0
December 31, 2015 • Arlington, Texas

DOMINATION

Crimson Tide Thump Spartans to Reach National Championship Game

They said they would be more focused, better prepared and show that they were hungry to play a championship, and then more than backed it up.

Looking like a team on a mission, the University of Alabama picked up were it left off at the SEC Championship and did what it does best at the Cotton Bowl: Dominate an opponent.

With senior quarterback Jake Coker completing 25 of 30 passes for 280 yards, and freshman wide receiver Calvin Ridley making eight catches for 138 yards and two touchdowns, Alabama rang in the New Year with a 38-0 thumping of Michigan State in a playoff semifinal.

Next up, the National Championship Game in Glendale, Ariz., where No. 2 Alabama would take on undefeated No. 1 Clemson.

"The focus that they had for this game was completely different than what we've ever had before," head coach Nick Saban said. "I think it paid off for them and we're looking forward to trying to do the same in the next game."

That focus stemmed in part from the previous year's disappointing showing in the playoffs, a 42-35 loss to Ohio State in the Sugar Bowl that Alabama vowed not to repeat.

But what made this victory so impressive was how the Crimson Tide (13-1) did so: While Michigan State tried to out-Alabama Alabama, the Crimson Tide instead out-Spartaned the Spartans.

In other words: All of the things that Michigan State was known for doing well Alabama simply did better. The Spartans spent most of the game with negative rushing yards and finished with only 29 on 26 carries. After having just 12 giveaways in their 13 games they lost the turnover battle. MSU even got outplayed on special teams.

The game was so lopsided that Alabama pulled its starters midway through the fourth quarter and still pulled off the impressive shutout.

"You never expect that against a good team like that," said junior linebacker Ryan Anderson, who had the first of Alabama's four sacks and two if its six tackles for a loss. "That's one of the best four teams in the country."

But it ran into probably the best defense, which looked as good as advertised. Michigan State reached the red zone (inside the 20) just once. Standout wide receiver Aaron Burbridge finished with just 39 yards and Jake Harbarger punted nine times.

≫≫ PLAY OF THE GAME

When senior linebacker Cyrus Jones picked off the pass at the Alabama 1-yard line at the end of the first half it was pretty much game over for Michigan State. The Spartans never made it back to the red zone.

Alabama receiver Calvin Ridley hauls in a long pass over Michigan State defensive back Demetrious Cox. Ridley finished with a team-leading eight receptions for 138 yards and two touchdowns, spurring the Crimson Tide to a 38-0 win.

"We come into every game with a mindset of dominating," said senior cornerback Cyrus Jones, who was named the defensive player of the game while Coker took home the offensive award. "We don't come in just trying to get by, we came in and wanted to stick it to them."

Although junior running back Derrick Henry had 46 carries against Auburn, and 44 versus Florida in the SEC Championship Game, Alabama came out going sideline-to-sideline with just about everyone else as Michigan State looked to shut the Heisman Trophy winner down.

That started to change midway through the second quarter, shortly after cornerback Darian Hicks took the brunt of a Henry hit and had to leave the game, when offensive coordinator Lanc Kiffin took a crack downfield. With freshman Ridley showing impressive closing speed he made the 50-yard catch and the rout was on.

With the equivalent of swinging a sledgehammer, Alabama subsequently put defensive linemen Jarran Reed and A'Shawn Robinson both in at fullback as Henry scored from 1-yard out—making up possibly the biggest backfield in college football history at 867 pounds.

It was Henry's 24th rushing touchdown of the season to set an SEC record and extended his streak of consecutive games with a rushing score to 19. He ended up with just 75 rushing yards, but went over 2,000 for the season and later added a second TD.

A 41-yard reception by junior tight end O.J. Howard helped Alabama extend the lead to 10-0 on a 47-yard field goal by junior kicker Adam Griffith, and with the Crimson Tide getting the ball to open the second half as well the pressure was on Michigan State to make something happen in the final 1:25 of the second quarter.

Connor Cook, who appeared to be getting frustrated over the numerous hits he was taking, completed four passes to move the Spartans into the red zone, but went to the well one time

Derrick Henry lunges into the end zone for one of his two touchdowns in Alabama's dominating victory over the Spartans.

too many and Jones made him pay with an interception at the Alabama 1.

"Totally my fault," Cook said. "I threw it short, obviously."

When Alabama opened the second half with a 75-yard drive and Ridley's 6-yard touchdown catch that had to be reviewed ("I knew my feet were in bounds, but I wasn't sure they thought I had the ball," he said) Michigan State had no choice but to turn the game over to Cook.

At one point cameras caught the senior quarterback walking to the sideline after a missed short pass and it was easy to read his lips: "They're (expletive) everywhere!" He completed 19 of 32 attempts for 210 yards and two interceptions.

"You could kind of sense their frustration a little bit," Jones said. "I could see it in their faces and it definitely gave us a little bit more hunger to keep going after them knowing that they're getting affected by what we're doing."

Any doubt about the outcome vanished with 3:24 remaining in the third quarter, when Jones juked out a defender on the sideline en route to a 57-yard touchdown on a punt return. Not only was it his fourth punt return for a score this season, and made it 24-0, but started provoking flashbacks of the last time these two teams met: The Crimson Tide's 49-7 victory in the Capital One Bowl at the end of the 2010 season.

That beat-down only sparked Alabama's back-to-back championship runs in 2011 and 2012. This time its hoping it will help get "one more," as the Crimson Tide players were saying in the throng of the postgame celebration on the field at AT&T Stadium.

One more win for another ring, which would be Saban's fifth and the program's 16th. One more for the defense to go down as one of the greatest in Crimson Tide history. One more game for everything ...

"We just want to go out on top," senior linebacker Dillon Lee said. ◼

Nick Saban and his players celebrate with the Goodyear Cotton Bowl Trophy. Alabama advanced to face Clemson in the College Football Playoff National Championship Game.

Alabama quarterback Jake Coker throws as pass during the shutout victory over Michigan State. Coker had a terrific and efficient game, finishing 25 for 30 with 286 passing yards and two touchdowns.

Alabama players celebrate after defeating Michigan State in the Cotton Bowl to advance to the College Football Playoff National Championship Game.